GET MOMENTUM

GET MOMENTUM

Your Ultimate Guide to Create $100k in 100 Days Without Fear, Overwhelm and Burnout

PENNY ELLIOTT

Get Momentum—the Woo with the Doo.
The perfect mix of mindset and strategy to have fast success in your
business so you can finally live your best life.

Get Momentum - Your Ultimate Guide to Create $100k in 100 Days Without Fear, Overwhelm and Burnout

First paperback edition December 2019

For print or media interviews with Penny, please contact
info@pennyelliott.com

Book design by Racheal Cox
Cover design by Christos Angelidakis
Edited by Lizette Balsdon

ISBN

Softcover 978-0-473-50636-0
Hardcover 978-0-473-50637-7
Kindle 978-0-473-50638-4

www.pennyelliott.com

YOUR FREE GIFT!

To get the best experience with this book, download the *Get Momentum Workbook* to work through your mindset and strategy for your personalised plan to implement $100k in 100 Days without fear, overwhelm and burnout.

You can grab a copy here:
www.pennyelliott.com/book

Rave Reviews From the Get Momentum Masterminders

Before I joined the Get Momentum Mastermind I didn't know how to grow my online courses and coaching business. I was stuck struggling to earn more than £2k months.

I knew there were two things limiting my business - not enough leads and not closing the sales on the calls.

The Get Momentum Mastermind solves this problem. I discovered exactly how to attract hundreds of more qualified leads in to my business and most importantly now convert more than 60% of my sales calls.

Most significantly I've been able to maintain my income whilst reducing my work days from 5 to 2 days a week, since having my daughter.

- KAT LUCKOCK, IMPACT STRATEGIST & BUSINESS COACH FOR SOCIAL ENTREPRENEURS, UK

Penny's Get Momentum Mastermind helped me to become more focused and determined to make by business succeed.

Her knowledge of business practices enabled me to run 2 successful overseas yoga retreats during my time on the program, plus build my private 1:1 clientele, complete and launch my first online course and run well received workshops.

This momentum has continued, with new retreats planned, and selling, for the new year, as well regular classes, workshops and online experiences. And all this whilst living in a small, remote community.

Penny and her Get Momentum Mastermind has been an integral part of my success, and I'm sure I would not be where I am now without her expertise.

- CASSANDRA PICKEL, INNER POWER YOGA, EXMOUTH, WESTERN AUSTRALIA

I had the pleasure of working with Penny as a business coach when I started to work in my custom cake business full time.

She is a wealth of knowledge and skills when it comes to anything business related. Penny had great ideas to help me market by new business and tips on bringing in new customers and sales. I was fully booked in no time!

Penny was also had great strategies for business growth without seeming pushy which I loved! Thoroughly recommend working with Penny to anyone wishing to get momentum in their business.

- JESSICA KEEN,
FOUNDER AND HEAD CAKE MAKER AT HEY SUGAR

I have been working with Penny in the Get Momentum Mastermind for the last five months and my business has been boosted into a completely different stratosphere of momentum.

I am now making money! I have clients! I have a website which I created myself that I love and can amend as and when I choose to. I have systems of automation in place which are allowing me to expand in different directions. I have structures that make sense and are working for me to be able to see a much bigger picture as to where my business can and is going. I have the confidence and passion to keep moving forward with the total support, information and encouragement that I have gained from Penny through the program.

- JACQLIN RICHARDS, PARENT MENTOR AND PATHWAYS
FACILITATOR AT YOUR PARENT JOURNEY

Dedicated to my son Joshua Jensen Elliott.

Remember my little monkey – anything is possible if you put your mind to it!

Table of Contents

Introduction

Money is something we all need to survive; a made-up bit of paper—or more recently, electronic number—that determines how we think, act, and feel. No matter how spiritual you are, you can't hide from the fact that privilege comes with money. It might not make you happier, but it sure does make life a bit easier when you can afford the things you love in life.

Yet, no-one likes to talk about money. In fact, you probably have a paper bag around this book if you're reading it in public, because how dare anyone see that you're reading about how to make $100k in 100 days. To some people, that might be downright outrageous and to others, that might be spare change and embarrassing to only be at the 6-figure mark.

Wherever you are on the spectrum, you've picked up this book to make your life better, and to finally get the shit you want—be it a new car, pay off the mortgage, or go on holiday. Heck, it might even be to provide better food for your kids!

I get it. I have been there before.

All I wanted was to have a successful business to build my own wealth for myself. Yep, just for me. I wanted to feel the huge amount of pride of doing it while still staying healthy and not losing it all repeating a deep-rooted family tradition.

Money has been on my mind since I was five-years old. Most children don't have to think about it, but I was forced to. I remember hiding in the bathroom as our house was repossessed. Imagine being a young child, tearful and fearful, while a stranger banged down your door to take your house away. It's safe to say that everything changed for me after that experience.

From that moment, I knew I never wanted to be in a place of lack again.

I wanted to make my own money, so that my security was never again dependent on the decisions of others. I wanted to be able to live the life that I desired, without fear or hesitation, and I wasn't going to repeat my family patterns.

As I grew up, I continued to ride the money rollercoaster, thanks to my father. I wanted to be able to depend on creating my own consistent income so that I could have stability and freedom in my life, but money seemed to be fleeting, and I never knew what was around the corner. However I was determined to build a more positive relationship with money.

When I graduated from University at 21, I decided that I would no longer have any negative thoughts about money. Instead, I would embrace it, create it, and celebrate it! With my Masters degree, I was determined to succeed. I took a sales role and committed to bringing more and more money into my life!

I wanted to have a positive relationship with money and to break free of any feelings of fear associated with money. Sales put me in the driver's seat. Sales woke up the side of me that is achievement-oriented, and gave me a way to help others improve their lives, too.

My new reality was meeting exciting people regularly and changing their lives dramatically—I loved every second! As a bonus, I got to stay in six-star resorts during work conferences. Worldwide travel became my norm. The drive and determination fuelled my fitness passion and gave me a mindset of steel.

What I've realized from over twenty years (I know, I know—don't look that old!) and over $15 million in sales, is that making money isn't difficult! And there's more than enough for everyone. Trust me, that's not something I believed when my dad defaulted on my private school payments, but it's true.

Now, my mission in life is to support women, just like you, in knowing that you can crush any goal you set your mind to! And specifically, to make $100k in 100 Days following in the exact footsteps I did.

You can run the business of your dreams, convert cold traffic into clients, and not feel nervous or sleazy when you get on a sales call.

You can be completely comfortable talking about money! And you can do it without having to hustle (one of my least favourite words, sorry Gary Vaynerchuk) or burn the midnight oil!

The goal is not to get to the retirement home and be wishing you had done things differently. Wouldn't you rather be the woman racing Zimmer frames and coaching the activities coordinator on her business?

So, let's dive on in as I show you how you can achieve $100k in 100 Days without working every hour under the sun and suffering from overwhelm and burnout; how to create wealth in terms of money in the bank without being a rich bitch that no-one likes. How to be happy, healthy, and wealthy— because it is possible and this book will show you exactly how.

I love it when people highlight, write comments and really use this book as a reference book for your life and business. The only thing I must say is, please do not fold the corner of the page over. That is blasphemy in any book world. But, if that means that you will come back to the page then that is fine, just don't tell me. ;)

Enjoy, be like a sponge and absorb it, and then, most importantly—implement your learning so you can get momentum and have the life you've always wanted.

SECTION 1:

Mindset—The Woo

Starting your own business is exciting. It can be one of the most joyful occasions of your life. You have an idea. You see a gap in the market and know you can fill it with your wonderful idea. You have a few drinks with a girlfriend and blurt out that you want to 'give it a go' and just like that, your formulated idea is out in the open.

Much like giving up smoking or going on a diet, as soon as you say it aloud, you're committed. You're what Ironman World Champ Chrissy Wellington says 'quids in'. People start to ask you how it's going, or remind you 'haven't you already quit smoking' when you light up a sneaky fag at a party a few Proseccos in.

The incestuous googling starts, and this is where the wheels start to spin being busy 'setting up' your business. There is so much to do and decide on. A website, a logo, a colour scheme, and—heck, do you use your name for the company or some clever name?

Before you know it, you're either so overwhelmed that you give up, or everything takes so long, you're embarrassed to keep going and talking about it. Much like a new boyfriend, the sparkle wears off and you're having to decide whether you stick with him, give the relationship the hard yards, or realise he's a dud and move on.

Good news. You've picked up the right book as I'm here to show *you* how to keep the sparkle alive in your business and keep them the hot lover you first fell for.

We start with the Woo first and for some of you this may be super frustrating as you just want to get on to the Doo section where you feel you'll actually get the results. I was the same too when I joined my first group program. But what I quickly came to realise was that without a rock solid mindset that was free of limiting beliefs and money blocks I wasn't going to have the business of my dreams, let alone the life of my dreams.

Business is 80% mindset and 20% strategy. Yet so many focus only on the strategy and then wonder why they can't fill their group programs or a very common one, why they have a roller coaster relationship with their finances. One month is great and then the next three are dreadful. This can all be down to mindset and the vibe you're putting out in to the world. Woo woo, I know. I was such a non-believer, too.

Yet, once I started to work on my mindset every single day, my business grew and not just a little bit but A LOT! So dive in to the chapters that follow with an open heart and a sense of experimentation. Don't knock it until you try it right?

Strap in and keep the pages turning. Lock in the highlighter (pink is the preferred colour!) and let's get your idea and business out to the world.

Because if you have the idea in you, it is there for a reason. The reason is not to be taken to the grave with you. It is time to flourish, my friend!

CHAPTER 1:

What do you Really Want to Achieve?

To keep the dream alive and turning into a reality, I want you to start with the end in mind.

What do you really want to achieve? I mean deep down?

And don't be afraid to say money, 'cos we all love money, just some of us are afraid to admit it and say it aloud. Don't worry, you're not a greedy witch. Behind the love for money, will be the real reason you want to have your own business and create the life you've always wanted. Together we'll find that and make it all OK to say, 'I love money flowing to me'.

As you may be aware, I love the outdoors and being outside. If I could strap my laptop to my chest like the ladies selling hot dogs at the ball games and be able to run and type, I would be in heaven. I love running and triathlon so much that I have done eighteen Ironman competitions and over forty marathons.

The Ironman World Champs in Kona, Hawaii was always my goal. I dreamed of swimming the 3.8km swim above the turtles in the bay, riding out in the hot lava fields on the 180km bike course, and then running the marathon out and back to Energy Lab—which, by the way, is anything BUT energetic. A story for a later time.

I held this dream for nine years and completed seventeen Ironmans before I qualified and made the race. Ninety-six thousand people race in ninety events around the globe throughout the year for one of the two-thousand five-hundred places in the world championship race; only 28% are female.

Over the nine years, I came so close to qualifying many times. I came fifth in my age group four times. Each time I had given my all, not only in the race, but in the months of training preceding the big day. I sat at the prize giving hoping the Kona slot would roll down to me, if someone above me didn't want her place. It never happened.

I was so lean and fast in some races, and raced in the ten-hour mark, giving me 'Ironman All World Athlete Gold Status'; awarded to the top one percent in the world. But the other girls had gone faster; conditions were perfect, and again, I didn't get one of the slots to be on the pier ready to race Kona that year.

Was I disappointed—OF COURSE! I cried every time, feeling dejected, disappointed, and ashamed. I spent the next two weeks downing red wine and dark chocolate until I felt ill from it.

Did I give up? No. I kept the end goal in mind ALWAYS. Nothing was going to stop me from getting that Ironman World Championship medal. Side note, I am obsessed by medals…

I never did qualify the traditional way through a qualifying race. In the end, I got what was called a Legacy Spot; a new program for athletes that had done twelve or more Ironmans. I got a starting spot the second year of the program being open, and crossing that Kona finish line was the best day of my life.

Why?

Because I kept the end in mind and didn't worry about the how. I just showed up every day to training and did my best. I'm obsessed with the details, knowing what would make me go faster—either equipment, training, nutrition, or mindset. I was obsessed with the end goal. I knew that I would get there in the end. I could feel it in my soul. It took nine bloody years, but I got there.

Coming into running my own business, I applied the same principles, and you can, too.

When I set the audacious goal—well I thought it was an audacious goal—of generating $100k in sales in 100 days, I totally got stuck on the how.

How could I generate that amount of money in such a short time? I mean, I had never done that much before, let alone in such a short time frame. I certainly didn't want to give up my triathlon or my relationship with my husband to hustle my ass off.

Just how would I do it? You might be thinking the same.

I went all out, living it every way possible; yet, it still seemed audacious.

But I knew I had come up with that number for a reason. It was inside me and therefore, had to come true.

You see, I desired to help women lose the 'little girl voice' when it came to growing their business. When I was in the corporate world, I saw men plainly stating their prices in negotiations. Then, when I moved into the online world, I heard women talking about their pricing, but they lost their tone, vibe, and even cowered when saying their prices. I wanted to inspire women's confidence in themselves and their value so they could get paid their worth and not work the crazy hours that were being spouted on the internet. The Badge of "80-100-hour weeks" in my eyes was neither needed, nor healthy! I wanted them to have both—financial independence and freedom to enjoy it. I've always had that and wanted to install this power in to women who deserved it!

Yet, no-one believed that you could be fit, healthy, have a growing business, and be profitable at the same time. I kept hearing, 'Surely, you have to work hard to make big money. You need to hustle, make multiple offers, and wear yourself out at networking events.' and so, when I did my first ever group program launch their words rang true - no one came. No one registered for my first group program. Well, one girl did. Yet in my eyes, the launch was one big flop.

I felt deflated and like a total failure. Sound familiar? It was my Ironman races all over again. Who was I to help women grow their business by stepping into their power when, here I was, powerless and in a bucket of despair? I had invested all my time and money into this launch and came out broke, exhausted, and quite frankly, ashamed. This was such a public launch, and here I had one person. So embarrassing.

Underneath all the disappointment was deep shame. You see, all my peers in my fancy high ticket Mastermind had launched programs that were crushing multiple five and even six figures. Here I was, not even hitting four figures. WTF?! HOW had this happened to me? How had this uber competitive person who trained her butt off to advance in the Ironman world, who has a 3.05 marathon time, went to University at 16 years old, be the biggest loser in her Mastermind?

I decided to leave the Mastermind and go with a new coach to get a new perspective; one that supported my goal of being in momentum by marrying the mindset and strategy. I reinvested and decided to do whatever she said to do. No matter how much I hated it, I would do it.

I took the Ironman approach—if I had to get in to a wind tunnel and sweat for six hours testing to go faster on the bike, I would do it. I applied the same principles to my business. I decided if she said write a certain way, I would. If she said raise your prices, I would. If she said delete something from my business, I would.

This was my last shot at keeping my business open. My last shot at helping all those women I knew I was put on the planet for. This was my last shot at becoming the success in business that I knew I was capable of being; that powerful woman I knew I was.

We set out to make 90k in 90 Days. I did EVERYTHING I was told to do. I also entered an Ironman 70.3. For the next 90 Days all I focused on was my business, training, and my new marriage. I had tunnel vision. The blinkers were on.

Eighty-five days came and I was short of the $90k goal. I had also booked a celebration holiday starting on the 90th day in Australia. Eighty-nine days rolled over, and while there were sales in the pipeline, none were committing. Ninety days came and I had fallen short—only by a few thousand, but I hadn't reached the finish line. I wasn't feeling financially flush or free... I was rushed and feeling the pressure!

Oh no, I had failed again. Fuck.

But the determination in me wouldn't let this challenge die, and instead of pulling out of the race, I just moved the finish line a wee bit. I raised the bar to $100k and moved the finish to 100 days—sounds better anyway, right?

And in the next ten days, the money came in and then some... I had done over six figures in 100 days.

I felt sooooo proud. Yes, there was money coming in, and I could sleep each night. Yes, I hammered the Ironman 70.3 with my loving husband at the finish line, and I had a blast. But most of all, I felt that sense of arriving, I had finally MADE it. I had a successful business and was helping hundreds of women on their way to creating that business and success feeling, too.

Best of all, I never worked over forty hours a week during those one-hundred days AND I trained over ten hours each week, outside in nature. I truly embodied my version of the get momentum lifestyle.

I can now continue helping women and give so much more than I did before. Every day is fulfilling and empowering. I live in momentum and keep moving forward feeling confident.

Can you see how focusing on the end goal was the driver and motivation the whole way, despite the setbacks in both Ironman and business? I never focused on the how when designing my goal as I would have dulled it down to a level I knew I had the how to achieve.

I now want you to spend the next ten minutes thinking about where you truly want to go and don't worry about how. I'd like to say spend the next three hours journaling on it, but let's be honest; you'd rather not do it, and skip this step altogether. That's not ideal, because if you don't know the end holiday destination how can you drive there?

Or you'd spend three hours writing out your end destination and not pick up this book again. Meaning you wouldn't find out how to get past knowing what your dream is! Not ideal, either!

So, start the timer. Ten minutes and GO!

Write on this page if you want to—smash it out! The first thing that comes to mind is what we're looking for. Or jump on over to the free workbook that comes with this book at www.pennyelliott.com/book and use the prompts there. Not the perfectly-manicured, conscious 'I think I can' goals. We want the big, hairy ones that sit in your subconscious that you blurt out and wonder where it came from.

Remember to forget the how and focus on what you really want to achieve and why.

Go for it!

GET MOMENTUM KEY POINTS

1. Almost everyone fails (sometimes several times) before achieving their goals.
2. Find a mentor to help you marry goals with strategy and mindset and push you to work hard to achieve them.
3. Write down your biggest, hairiest goal that scares you shitless.

Chapter 2:

Now You Have Your Goal.
Does it Scare You Shitless?

Now you know where you're going, it's important to have the confidence to be able to go for that goal. Often, it's hard enough just to find the goal, let alone have the confidence to go for it and to continue to keep that confidence.

Before I dive into the how-tos, I want to tell you a little story... As you may know, I'm really into Ironman Triathlon; but when I first decided to do an Ironman, I'd not even run a half marathon, let alone a marathon. I had not done any *real* training. In fact, I was actually more of a late night party girl. For me to be able to run to the letterbox and back again was hard enough, let alone trying to go for an Ironman finish.

As you may imagine, when I told my friends I was going to do the Ironman, they kind of chuckled and said, "What, between bottles of wine?" So, I decided it was time to give this a go. The determination came out in me!

Instead of trying to do it on my own, I sat down, and I thought, "Right, what is going to be the hardest things about achieving this 'Ironman' distance; a 3.8-kilometer swim, 180-kilometer bike ride, and a marathon?" I knew that if my mind could tell my body that it could do it, I would be there. I needed a plan, a team and commitment.

The first person I enlisted in my team of people to help me reach that elusive finish line was a sports psychologist, because I know the body will go where the mind will take it. So, I spent my first amount of time with a sports psychologist learning how to train my mind to stay focused for what could potentially be a fifteen-hour day. I needed to learn how to handle the lows and what to do to stop race day jitters.

I then enlisted the help of a nutritionist, gorgeous Nikki Hart, because I knew that if my body wasn't fuelled correctly, I wasn't going to be able to make it to the finish line, no matter how hard my brain decided it wanted to get there. You must have the fuel in the tank to be able to get to the finish line.

Thirdly, I hired a coach. I knew that I didn't know enough about training for a distance this far; what it would take and how many hours or how many minutes or how fast I needed to be, or how many hours a week I needed to put into training. The unknowns went on and on. I didn't want to over train, and I certainly didn't want to arrive on the start line completely undertrained for this distance. So, I hired myself a coach who had years of experience both as a professional athlete and coaching hundreds of newbies like myself; Canadian Frank Clarke.

The fourth thing I did was surrounding myself with like-minded people. I didn't want my friends saying to me, "What, between bottles of wine?" I wanted to be around other people that didn't say, "Oh my gosh, you're crazy," when I said I was going on a 5 hours bike ride on Saturday morning.

I wanted them to say, "Oh my goodness, you're crazy" in the right kinda crazy way. I wanted to be with people that would be excited and say, "Hey, come and do this event. Come and do that event. This is how you wear your cycling shorts, and by the way, it's not over a pair of underpants, if that's what you've done in the past. This is what you do when you have your period, and you've still gotta train." Silly little things like this can totally derail you when you're training for such a big event.

Having people around you, surrounding you, and the confidence that that builds within you—being able to ask those silly little questions, being able to know that when my brain was about to give out. I knew the techniques to pull myself back in line.

When I wanted to go and eat McDonald's and have four or five glasses of wine at a barbecue, I knew what it would do to me the next day in my training, so I didn't do that. When I wanted to stay in bed on Sunday morning, I knew that my coach would be waiting for me, ready to do that run with me, and to make sure I had the run distance to be able to reach the marathon finish line.

The fifth and final thing that I did that is so important is, I entered. I paid for my accommodation down in Taupo, New Zealand—a beautiful area of the world—and I paid my entry fee of $800. I committed 100% to this goal.

Now, you might be thinking, "Well, that's great in sport, but how does it pertain to business?" Well, when you think about the goal that you set in Chapter 1, the big dream goal, I now want you to break it down.

Do you have the mental strength that goes with running a business? Do you need to sharpen your mindset? Do you need a mindset coach?

Have you got the nutrition sorted? You can't run a business if you are eating crap. You will have crap output. Where do you need to up your nutrition game?

Have you got the coach with you that has done it before, that knows just how far to push something and equally just how far not to? Do you know how much sales speak you need and how much marketing to put in? (If you don't, don't worry. This book will continue to tell you how to do that in the "Doo" section.)

Are you surrounded by likeminded people that lift you up? People who support your big dream and encourage you? Because this is so important. When your family don't really understand what's going on, you have like-minded mastermind buddies to be able to chat with. These are the people with whom you can throw ideas around and know that bad days are just a day, and it will all come good.

And finally, have you committed 100% to the goal? Are you boots in? And as the English say, 'Are you quids in?', i.e., have you paid? Have you bought into it? Are you definitely going there 100%? There's no turning back. Burn the boats as famous business coach James Wedmore says.

When I first started out in this online entrepreneurial world, I wanted to work with men and women, and I realized just how many women were bringing out a *Little Girl Voice* when it came to their business. They were very excited about the prospect of having their own business, and this might be you right now, but when somebody asks you what is it that you do, they brought out, "Oh well, just um, well um, oh, I *just* bake cakes,"," or "Oh well, you know, I'm *just* a yoga teacher." They brought out this really tiny little girl voice and weren't confident about talking about what they do.

Seeing this timidity was my catalyst for really helping female entrepreneurs, just like yourself, be bold and go for gold to hit those $100k goals in 100 days. That's exactly what we do in the Get Momentum Mastermind. We help women gain their confidence, to be able to say what they do with pride. Removing the 'just'.

So, what I want you to do is complete this little exercise to identify where you need help and support moving forward to achieve your dream. Use the free workbook at www.pennyelliott.com/book to give yourself the space to jot your answers down.

1. Is your mindset clear? Do you need help with that?
2. Do you have your nutrition and your sleep and your hydration dialled in?
3. Do you have a coach onboard who can show you the fastest path to success in your field?
4. Have you financially committed yourself?
5. Are you surrounding yourself with the right people?

The first one to four are pretty easy to buy and purchase and make yourself do. For example, my *Get Momentum Mastermind* helps you stay on track with weekly mindset, hydration, nutrition, and fitness coaching. You receive business group coaching, along with weekly masterclasses and documentation on how to grow your business successfully online.

But it's surrounding yourself with the right type of people that makes a HUGE difference, and that's how you gain the confidence to go for that goal that scares you shitless. In a mastermind or entrepreneurial group, you're surrounding yourself with other people who are also going for goals that scare them shitless, and so you can be scared shitless together. As soon as you are scared shitless with someone else, it normalizes the whole experience and means that you can feel a whole lot more confident in yourself going for that big goal.

When you surround yourself with these new people, you create your new identity, and your new identity is going for this dream goal, this big goal, right? That might mean that you need to cut out some negative people. Hard, but fair. To simplify identifying these negative nellies, grab yourself a sheet of paper and draw a circle in the middle, put the word 'me' in it. Or if you're fancy, draw a picture of yourself. So that's you—not me, you, just to be clear.

Around the 'me', put the people who are the closest to you who are positive and supportive of your goals. Then do another circle around the outside of that, and put the people who are less supportive, but are still quite supportive of your goals. Outside the last circle, put all the people that are negative to you, make fun of you and your ambition, or are just plain mean.

Now, it might be really difficult, because you might have your mum, your dad, or your spouse in that very far outer circle. While I don't advise cutting them off completely if they are a very close relative, I do advise having minimal time with them talking about your business and where you're going, especially when you're first starting out. You cannot have anyone putting any doubt into your mind, because you need to keep the faith and program your mindset to be strong. When you have wavering support, it makes it very, very difficult to keep your mind strong and in the game.

So, you want to keep the ones that are in your close circle very close to you and the ones that are on the outside, on the outside. It is a very easy graphical way to work out who is supportive of you in this journey and who isn't.

You might be thinking (and visually seeing!) there's nobody in your inner circle who is super supportive, and if that's the case, I want you to find a group or a mastermind that you can join that supports you in your momentum to your big dream goal. This can either be in your industry, females, or with a coach whom you really enjoy working with, so that you can get that support you deserve. This is how you grow that inner circle that is really close to you. You gain confidence through seeing them being able to do the things that you want to do, and they see things that you're doing that give them confidence, and it feeds off each other. It's a beautiful circle of solid support right around you.

GET MOMENTUM KEY POINTS

1. You can achieve great things even if you have no experience at all. It's a matter of implementing a team of support people and financially committing.
2. Commit to your goal with absolute certainty and speak it with confidence.
3. Surround yourself by people who uplift and support you every step of the way.

CHAPTER 3:

But What About Being Seen as a Rich Bitch? Money Blocks and You.

It's all good and well to say, Yep, I am going for this big dream and I am now surrounding myself with the support and people to make me confident when there is a little demon in the back of your head saying, "But, what if I make it? What will people think of me then?"

Consciously, we all want to be rich—either money, or time, or love. Or all three. Whichever it is, we all want it. Those who say 'I don't care about money; I just want to be happy'— I challenge them to say what is really going on in their subconscious. You wouldn't have brought this book if you weren't a teensy tiniest bit interested in being rich!

However, in all of us is the desire to be liked. As babies, our first interaction is a smile; when we get a smile back, we know we are liked and loved. While our conscious brain is saying 'Yep, show me the money' like on the Jerry Maguire movie, our subconscious goes haywire.

"What if I make all this money and don't know what to do with it?"

"What if I make all this money and become a rich bitch that no one likes?"

"What if I have more money than my family and they ostracise me?"

"What if I'm expected to pay for everything?"

Where do all these subconscious thoughts come from? Because you know you wouldn't be nasty with your wealth and would be giving and loving with all your money. So, where do these bad money thoughts creep in from?

We need to take a step back to your childhood, and dig deep. Warning: this could get ugly!

But before we deep dive and find what filled your head with rot about money being evil, I want to share a story with you to show you just how influenced we are at such a young age.

My Dad went bankrupt when I was five years old. To add salt to the wound he was cheating on my mum with his secretary, so in vouge for the early 80's. He went to the bank and forged my mum's signature and took all her savings, some of which was set aside to take me to Disneyland. He left mum and I with no money, no home, not even a car to drive to school in. He went to live with his secretary and I never saw him again for over 2 years.

From that moment, I knew I never wanted to be in a place of such destitute as my mother was. She had worked for my father, trusted him with all the financials and never doubted he would love after us as a family. The seed was planted firmly in me to be a financially independent gal.

This was then reinforced when I was plucked from Boarding School two weeks shy of my year end exams as my boarding school fees hadn't been paid…the entire year! My father had said he was paying the tuition but in fact my Grammy had been giving him the money to pay and he had spent the year on his latest mistress. I was again victim to being on the roller coaster of money.

When I graduated from University, I decided that I would no longer have any negative thoughts about money. Instead, I would embrace it, create it, and celebrate it! I took a sales role and committed to bringing more and more money into my life! By working on my money mindset daily, I have been able to smooth the roller coaster out.

I want full disclosure here too; I am no money saint now. I still have highs and lows as I progress through life. Having a baby is the most recent opening of a can of money worms. But having the techniques to be able to work on these money blocks gives you the power to overcome any change.

You might find similar patterns in your life, too. Something that was said or done in your childhood that you thought

29

wasn't your problem yet, now you take a close look at it, you see yourself following the same pattern.

Bugger (kiwi slang for oh dang it)!

On a course I did, we looked at all these 'money blocks' in our past, for MONTHS. I dug up so many it almost became obsessional depressing. I could then use them as excuses for why I wasn't doing as well as I had hoped in my business.

After all, I had it drilled in to me that 'if I spent all my money I'd end up like my father', and no matter how hard I had tried, here I was, having a great month, investing it all back into the business to have the growth I was sure would come from investing, and then having some very lean months to follow. That roller coaster was showing up again.

It then hit me; kinda like the roller coaster threw me off! It's all good and well having money blocks, identifying them, and seeing them for what they are—blocks that you inherited and have been carrying around with you for your life. But how the fuck do you get rid of them?

I knew I did NOT want to be bankrupt like my father. I was SICK of being on the rollercoaster. I wanted steady growth in my business AND my bank accounts.

I'm guessing you do, too!

I want you to spend time identifying your money blocks. Take solitude here to really see the patterns and what they are. But don't stop there; it is now time to give them forgiveness and set them free. Forgiveness is the healer; it releases the emotion of the situation. You see, it is the emotion that you're holding onto and need to release in all of your money blocks.

To reach the forgiveness level, you need to accept that you had some small part in the problem, even at a vibrational level. This is the hard pill to swallow. I certainly did not want to admit I had anything to do with my father's money issues. But if I was honest with myself, I did. I was the usual kid that wanted the latest everything and that put pressure on him to twist more deals. Now, I know at five years old, I had no real way of knowing this, but I accept that I was part of the equation. Similarly, the investing in my business with expectation that would take me to the next level was my doing, and I needed to realise that I was part of that problem. Not nice, huh? There is an upside.

Now you have the icky part out of the way by owning your part in the block, you can do a ceremony of releasing these past money blocks to heal the emotions. It was first introduced to me by Denise Duffield-Thomas, author and amazing CEO of *Get Rich, Lucky Bitch*. She based it on the Hawaiian practice of reconciliation and forgiveness called Ho'oponopono. Who doesn't love Hawaii?!

Write out all your money blocks as sentences in a journal. Start from the very beginning; what is your first memory about money? Keep moving through your life. Get them all out. Was it that you felt poor going to school and not having the latest jelly shoes (those things just gave you blisters anyway!)? Or was it that you were embarrassed by your dad's big, fancy car and the kids making fun of you? Or was it at work when that one person never chipped in for the company gifts and you thought what a tight arse they were and resented them?

Get them all out! This can take all day and you might add to it as the week goes on.

That's OK.

Then leave the list for 24 hours.

Come back to it and go through each one. Sit with each one, go back to that time, feel in to each emotion and what that meant to you. Then say or write below the incident, "I forgive you. I'm sorry. And I love you."

Simple, yet VERY powerful.

Do this for each money block situation.

The apology releases the person or incident. You may not want to say sorry or let them get away with it—I know I sure didn't want to. Even if you're not 100% sorry, say it anyway as it will release you from the stranglehold of this money block That's what we're after here.

Saying I love you gives the cellular and soul healing to be able to move forward. Love is the most powerful tool in the Universe. By forgiving, being sorry, and loving, you're not saying it was OK what they did, or that they can do it again, you're just releasing the negative energy and allowing a more positive high vibration to flow in. Cool, huh?

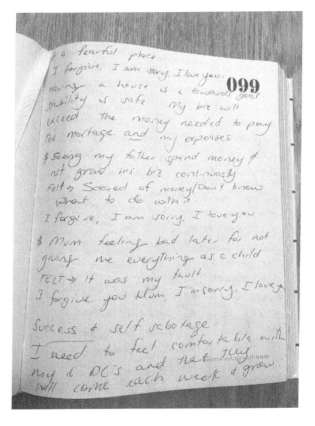

Now, if you want to take it next level woo (and why wouldn't you, because you might as well try everything when it comes to making more money, right?!) then I cannot recommend

EFT (Emotional Freedom Techniques) enough. Otherwise known as Tapping.

By tapping on the meridian lines, you can rewire your brain and energy fields to clear out the old money vibe and, most importantly, bring in the money story you want to live and breathe. Margaret M. Lynch is the guru in the Tapping field with her amazing book, *Tapping Into Wealth: How Emotional Freedom Techniques (EFT) Can Help You Clear the Path to Making More Money*. She has a background in science and mathematics—so on the other end of the woo spectrum! However, the tapping caught her eye as it is the only scientifically proven therapy to retrain the brain to think and function in a new way. So much so that practitioners use it in PTSD patients to remove the emotion of the horrific things they have experienced and seen from their brains.

By removing the emotion, you remove attachment to the situation. Think about a friend—we all have at least one— that looooveees drama! You know the one that even if she won the lottery, she'd find a reason to complain. These kinds of people are addicted to the drama. Addicted to the *emotion* of the situation. They love to relive it and stir up colourful emotions with it. You always leave lunch with them shaking your head and feeling like you endured the hour instead of enjoying the time spent with them.

This is what you're doing by holding onto the emotion with a money story. Unfortunately, in some light, that emotion and story are supporting you currently, too. For example, when I found out I was pregnant, I thought my whole business was going to go down the drain. I got all emotional about it, even more than you do when you're pregnant! I started to give up and not show up. It was also easier for me to not show up and then I didn't run the risk of failing too. When I dug deep with my coach, I could see that my mum had me and focused all her attention on me. While she kept farming, she didn't keep her money safe from my father. That was a money story that was triggered in me that hadn't been thought of until I too, became pregnant. I needed to clear that emotion and put in a new positive one. One where I was a Millionaire Mumma!

Can you see how the money block and emotion was supporting me? And why I needed to clear it?

To start tapping away your blocks and emotions is very easy. All you need is your head and your hand. Simple, ah? And you can do it anywhere and everywhere.

First, think of one of your money blocks. Let's use a money goal: to hit $100k in your business.

Write that big, hairy money goal down... I use a pink marker because it jumps off the page at me more!

Really stare at it.

Now, write down all the emotions that come up when you look at that number.

When working with clients, the most common first emotional answer is, "Yahoo! That would be awesome!" Then, "Who am I to make that much when I can't even make $5k right now? I don't deserve to make that much. I'd be a fraud. I'm not confident enough. Who would work with me for that?"

Whatever emotions come up, write them down.

Monitor how you feel on a scale of 1 to 10. Ten being strong emotions, such as I FEEL that and wanna cry, shout, and or hide.

Then, do the following exercise tapping your fingers on all the EFT points in order while saying the script below to clear those negative, nasty emotions. You can insert your own emotional words and goals in the free workbook with this book—www.pennyelliott.com/book. The great thing about EFT is that it doesn't have to be perfect to work.

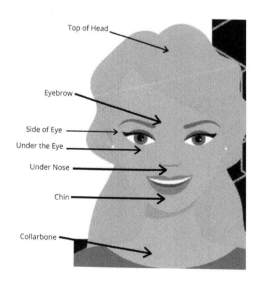

Tap through all the points, using the following phrases:

It's a big ol' goal!

It's too much for me.

I can't see how I could get to this much money.

It's a lot of money.

What could I possibly do to earn that amount?

Especially in such a short time frame.

Maybe it would be really hard.

It's almost crazy to earn that much.

I just can't imagine that amount of money.

What would I do with that amount anyway?

Why do I need that much?

It seems like it'd be really hard to earn that much.

It will probably be a LOT of work.

It's just too much and all too hard.

Take several deep breaths and see how you feel about this big goal now? If you still feel tense, repeat the round of tapping before moving on to the positive round.

Tap through all the points using the positive phrases…

I'm not so sure about this big goal.

I still think it will be hard work.

I choose to have faith.

That I will have integrity to my goal.

I am following my intention.

And my intention is

to step each day into my life's purpose with passion.

And with joy.

My intention is to become more of me
Than I have ever been.
My intention is to be surrounded by the people that bring me joy.
As I let go of my programming and beliefs
I am choosing to be open.
Beyond what I can currently see
I'm having faith.
That everything I need to accomplish this big goal
Will be right in front of me at exactly the right time.
It's pretty awesome how these things appear when they're needed.
Impossible things happen every day for me.
I am going to open myself up to the possibility.
And focus with positive intent.
Allowing it to come in to my reality.

Take a few deep breaths.

Now. think back to the big hairy number you wrote down (in pink) and see what emotions come up for you. On a scale of 1 to 10, where are they now? Keep doing the tapping round until you feel neutral emotions or even excitement about your goal.

GET MOMENTUM KEY POINTS

1. How do you REALLY feel about being rich? Discovering your blocks may hold the key to your success.

2. There are several tools to use to let go of your negative connotations to money that you have carried since you were a child.

3. You must let go of your unforgiveness towards people and situations that shaped your perceptions about money. The practice of Ho'oponopono and EFT can help with that!

CHAPTER 4:

Your New Lingo and How to Have Conscious Language

How you speak to yourself really matters. Like *really* matters. Now that you have these big dreams and goals, you're often your own worst enemy. How often do you sit back and think, "Oh I'd love to do that" and then this little voice pops up in your head that tells you, "Well, you've not been able to achieve that in the past, so why do you think you can now?" or "Well, life never works out that way for me, so why do I think it's gonna work this time?" Or my favourite; "Who am I to be able to actually achieve this?"

This little voice that pops up inside your head is actually one of the hardest things to remove, and it's also one of the hardest critics you'll ever have. It's not gonna be someone external. It's always someone in your own mind. It's time to kick this nasty bitch voice out of your head and into the curb. In this chapter, we're gonna dive into how to align your inner thoughts, your inner mind, and your conscious language so that you are speaking your dreams into fruition, without the nasty voice popping up!

I wanna tell you a little story to start with first. I've had the privilege of being coached by some extraordinary people in this world along my journey. One of the things that I always do, is invest in myself to be able to grow myself and my business, so then I can pass this on to my clients and readers like yourself.

I've always thought that I'm quite a bubbly, outgoing person. My report cards always spoke about how very vivacious, outspoken, and often disruptive I was to the rest of the class. It probably had something to do with the fact that I'd always be telling people, "Oh, you could do it this way, or you could do it that way" and giving them loads of advice and help.

However, on the inside, I'd always be telling myself a very different story. It's very easy to be able to tell someone else how they should do something or give them motivation. But when you're thinking of only yourself it's very difficult to swallow the same pill you're prescribing to someone else.

This was highlighted to me when I was being coached by an amazing chap called James Williams, who is married to Emily Williams, founder of *I Heart My Life*. James introduced me to a phenomenon brought around by Eckhart Tolle and his wonderful book. *The Power of Now* is very dry and I had to listen to it instead of reading the book, because I wanted to absorb the learnings and not fall asleep! It is read by Eckhart and so is far more enjoyable in my eyes.

You can speed up books on Audible, too, so they suit my pace of learning and absorption. In a nutshell, the whole concept of *The Power of Now* is about being present and staying in the present. So often, our inner voice spends too much time in either the past or the present, trying to predict what will happen in the future based on what we did in the past. A sure-fire way of getting what you've already had on repeat in the future.

Now Eckhart Tolle goes into it much deeper than this in his 236-page book. However, James Williams really summed it up for me nicely by saying that it's like you have three rooms; the Library, the Future Room, and the Present.

The Library is where all your past events or past experiences are stored from your life. So, this might be that you have tried to start a business before and it didn't work; that's a file in the previous library. It might be that you ran 5K and it went really well; that's another library file. It might be that you have tried to grow your social media following and it didn't work. Again, that's a previous file in your library.

Then you have the Future Room. This is where all your dreams and desires come from, which is what we've covered in the previous chapters. This is where you hold all your aspirations and all your desires. So, you have the Library, which is your history, your past. You have the Future Room, which is the room that you step into to create your dreams and desires.

However, the third room—the Present—is the room in which you want to spend the most amount of time, which is right here, right now. As soon as you've read it, that comment has now popped back into the Library. So, to be present, it's just here right now, now, now, and right now, and that's it.

The only thing that determines right NOW is what you are drawing on from your Library to push you forward to a Future Room. So, I'm gonna say that again: What determines next in your Present room is what you draw from in your Library to push you forward to your Future Room.

Now, James eloquently put it in the three different rooms which makes it feel so much easier than trying to always think, "I'm present. I'm present. I'm present. I'm present. Now, now, now, now, now." Where it becomes a helpful analogy is if you are trying to think about the now and you're drawing on negative sabotaging files from your previous library. If you're in this state then you can't push forward to your dreams and goals drawing from negativity.

For example, your dream might be to create a business that brings you five figures a month, every month. Right now, what are you doing to create that? If you're doing what you need to in the Present Room you are pushing forward to your dream five figures a month, that's your Future Room. But you might be drawing on a negative file from your Library like, "Well, that's never worked before. Who am I to have that kind of dream? I've never made that much money before, so how am I gonna do it now?" This self-chatter in your head is coming from your Library, your old life. Can you see how you pull from your Library Room in a negative way? And how sabotaging that voice is in your head to you being Present and striving for the Future room?

We're gonna talk about how you can change that lingo (in New Zealand lingo is a kiwi-ism for language), so that you're consciously bringing about what you want from your Future Room into your Present now. Without using any negative Library files. By doing that you'll be able to create, or manifest, or have alignment in the Universe. Draw that energy, that high vibration, into you just by using your lingo. How cool is that? Right? So simple. By changing a few words how you can manifest your life into what you desire. Your Future Room will become your present reality really quickly.

For example, I always like to use sports analogies to illustrate how principles work. The marathon is something that everyone aspires to run, and a while ago I got really serious about my running. I decided that I had done my Ironmans for the year, and if you don't know me, I've done 18 of these endurance long distance triathlons and about 40 marathons. Running is definitely my strength of the three disciplines of swim, bike, run. In 2012 I decided to focus heavily on running and just see how far I could push my training and race time.

Now, using conscious language 'I hope to finish' turns into 'I am finishing the marathon'. I wanted to hit a target time of sub three hours. Drawing from my Library would have meant the voice in my head was saying 'You'll finish, but you've never run that fast before, so I doubt you will this time.'

This is where the conscious language really comes to fruition. I had never run that fast before. Heck, I had never run that fast pace over 5K before. My fastest marathon at that point was about four hours. To cut an hour off a marathon is a lot of time! It's a 25% reduction in time when you're already at the pointy end of the deal. To put this in to perspective, according to marastats.com only 1% in the world get below three hours as a woman.

It was an audacious goal, but I really wanted to try and achieve the elusive sub-three. To get there, I needed to do a shed load of training AND I had to change my conscious language— both externally and in my head.

I started talking about how fast I ran instead of how much I had to achieve or how slow that run was. I had to say, "This run is improving. My runs are improving. I am improving every time. I am stronger. I am dropping weight to be lean and fast," and change all of my conscious language to reflect the person in the future who was crossing the line just under three hours.

Now, did I cross the line at three hours? I qualified to get a place in the New York Marathon, because I had run a fast-enough half marathon to be able to get a good for age spot.

That in itself is an achievement, and one of the stepping stones toward that Future Room.

I rocked up to the start line of the New York Marathon, and it was absolutely freezing. You get the ferry across to Staten Island and then into a bus to the start area. Everyone's laying about in their sleeping bags, waiting for the start. It's predawn, and—did I mention?—it's freezing! Loud music blares out to wake you up, and there's Dunkin Donuts coffee and bagels ready to go for all the athletes. Everyone's super nervous.

Here I am, dressed in about five different layers of clothing, sitting on a piece of newspaper in a plastic bag in my start pen to stop my butt checks freezing, two hours before the start time of 7am. I was sitting there waiting, and waiting, and waiting—freezing. I peeled off all my clothes just as we were about to get going, and ran over that first bridge from Staten Island. I was going so well. I was right on time. I ran my fastest half marathon as I went through the halfway mark. More importantly, I was just on target to hit my sub-three hours.

Once I reached Central Park, the route became a bit hillier; my legs weren't as strong as I had hoped they would be, and I dropped off the pace a little bit.

This is where conscious language really needed to come into play. I kept saying, "Come on! You've gotta hit this three-hour mark. You've gotta hit this three-hour mark. You've gotta go sub-three. You've gotta go sub-three."

I could have let the bitchy voice in; "Ha! I told you that you'd never run that fast! You're tired and it's all over." But I didn't.

I chanted to myself, "You're healthy and strong, you're healthy and strong" a bazillion times until that medal was hanging around my neck!

In the end, I ran a 3:12, which was an absolutely extraordinary time for me. That was about 48 minutes taken off my Personal Best of the marathon. I was ecstatic, but it wasn't sub-three.

So, I went away and celebrated. I bought myself a Tiffany's necklace and had the time engraved on the back. The next year, I entered the Berlin Marathon, which is a bit of faster, flatter marathon. It's where Eliud Kipchoge of Kenya broke the world record in 2018 in a lightning speed of 2.01.39. Side note, I wonder if he's peeved at that 1 minute and 39 seconds and chasing a sub-two?

I decided that I would go for sub-three again. Same story; big line-up, freezing cold start, and fading pace in the last kilometres. I finished in the top fifty non-professional women, though and I ran 3:05.35.

Another celebration, and this time an engraved Tiffany's ring, I reflected.

I thought, "What is going on here?" I went back to my sports psychology lessons and coaching that I'd had in the early days of my Ironman career. It hit me. My conscious language was good, but not quite right…

The reason I wasn't hitting the sub-three was because I kept telling my brain "three". Interestingly, our brain only hears the last thing that you say. I just kept saying "three", so my brain was going for three hours.

Therefore, if I want to go under three hours in a marathon time, I need to start telling my brain, "I will run two hours fifty-eight minutes," or "two hours fifty-seven," or "two hours forty-eight." —whatever that might be. But something with a two in the language, instead of a three.

You might be thinking, "You just needed to train harder. You needed to go faster. You needed to have a better start position, better nutrition…" And an element of that is true, but I was fit enough to definitely run two-something; it's just that I'd been telling myself three. So, I was getting close to three. But I wasn't telling myself two; my language wasn't supporting me. I had to be more conscious of what words I was using.

Now, you might be telling yourself in your business that you wanna hit five figures a month. So, you'll hit $10,000, $10,000, $10,000 each month and not a penny more. That's it, until you tell yourself you desire multiple five figures. You need to have specific conscious language about what you want.

Be consistent about your conscious language, too. You might do multiple five figures once, and then not again, and then once, and then not again. This can come from you speaking consciously one month and then being lax the next month. I want you to really look at your conscious language around making sure that when you're in you're -

1) In your Present Room, and

2) You're using conscious language to pull yourself towards your dreams that isn't taken from negative Library files.

Here's a list of examples of how you can be in the Present Room using conscious language. You'll be able to see from a more extensive list in the free workbook at www.pennyelliott.com/book and know exactly how you can change and tweak several words to manifest your dreams through your language.

Here are a few to get you going:

- I can't becomes I can
- I think becomes I am
- I should becomes I could
- I might becomes I will

The teaching from this is to only focus on NOW. I really want you to be hyper-vigilant and hyper-aware of what that's like.

What I want you to do is in the next 24 hours—either with a notepad, or your phone, or in the free workbook at www.pennyelliott.com/book—is to commit to yourself to write down all your thoughts.

This can be quite painful, especially dragging your notebook out each time you have a thought. So, you can use your phone to write it down. But set alarm reminders in your phone so that you are consciously coming back to the exercise and actually writing your thoughts down. I'll admit, I've tried to do this many times, and completely forgotten. Then, my inner critic has said to me, "Oh, I can't believe you couldn't even do 24 hours." Which again, is clearly unhelpful and that awful little voice inside your head.

At the end of that twenty-four hours, I want you to go through your notes and assess it, and think to yourself, "If I was my best friend, would I be saying these things to her?" I can guarantee you, you would not be so cruel and harsh to your best friend. You would be saying *much* nicer things. This exercise will highlight to you exactly how you need to be so much nicer to yourself and much more positive, using conscious language. It will also show you just how hard it is to be focused for twenty-four hours! Oh, how we've become a goldfish world—but that rant is a another book!

I suggest you now go through and re-write all of the nasty things that you said to yourself in positive, conscious language. Let me know in the *Get Momentum Entrepreneurs Facebook Group* how you are getting on and what transformations you have made from your unconscious to conscious language.

I would love to hear from you. I love hearing the transformations. From this you'll be able to easily manifest those dreams and desires that we started to talk about in the previous chapters.

They always start to come through as smaller manifestations to start with, and then suddenly, you will have this amazing leap. It is quite incredible just how tweaking some simple, small words can make such a massive difference.

GET MOMENTUM KEY POINTS

1. If you want your big goals to materialise, you need to be conscious of your inner voice.
2. Your self-talk comes from files from your Past Library. You must re-train your inner voice to achieve new goals set in the Future Room.
3. Make your goals extremely specific, focus on what you want and not what you don't want.

CHAPTER 5:

Fresh Air, Movement, Connecting to Source, Hydration and Sleep - Looking After You

Now that you have your big dreams sorted and you're speaking to yourself in a positive way, it's important to understand that **you** are your business. Now, you might have staff, or not. Most people will start as a solopreneur; even people like Steve Jobs, and Russell Brunson started as one person. Yet that one person is so critical in keeping the business moving forward. Look at Apple for example; when Steve Jobs passed away at such an early age, the company struggled to keep moving forward at the same rate without him at the helm, despite having a huge team. Apple has changed and hasn't brought out any new products (at the point of writing this) that have drastically changed the shape and trajectory of how we consume media, music, and the internet, without his leadership and vision. This may change in the future but what I'm trying to highlight here is the fact that your health needs to be the number one priority in order to run your business.

YOU are your business.

Unfortunately, I see people putting health very low down on the scale of daily importance.

Many entrepreneurs spend a lot of time creating funnels, creating ads, which is all very, very important for creating $100k in 100 days. But if you are sick in bed, or even in hospital with burnout or any symptoms of burnout like a cold, a sniffly nose, migraines, depression, ulcers, zits, or aching body parts, then you're on a slippery slope to closing your business. As the saying goes, you're working yourself into the ground, which means that you cannot be in your business and you cannot run it.

You might think, 'Oh, Penny, you're so dramatic and it doesn't apply to me. I have staff that can run my business'. But they need the leader. They need leadership, and the person to provide it is you.

So, it's very important to put your health above everything else. To be able to reach you big goal and from now on in this book we will us the goal of $100k in 100 days, your health needs to be a top priority—not just once a week either. Going to the gym on a Saturday morning, or going for a run on a Thursday night once a week is great, but it's not going to keep you healthy for the other six out of seven days.

Most people are really, really healthy on a Monday, and by Sunday they're back on the junk food and couch. It's this up and down cycle that creates poor health habits. What we're aiming to do, every single day for the 100 days (and beyond), is to put your health and wellbeing first *and* being outside for your exercise.

Why outside? Plenty of research supports the fact that being outside while sweating and connecting to our natural source has a calming effect on the body and brain. That means you're looking after your inner health on a cellular and spiritual level. Two birds, one stone. #timehack

Before I go into detail on how you can achieve this, I want to tell you a little bit of a story about my first journey to $100k in 100 days and how I put my health first, despite what the advisors said. I was completely adamant that I was not going to lose my fitness during this time. I had been part of a high-level mastermind—we're talking multiple five figure payments; it was a big deal for me to stretch myself that far. On every call I received the message, "Well if you're going to be serious about your business, you need to drop this triathlon training fantasy."

I was determined to prove that you can have the business and sleep 8 hours a night; that you can make $100k in 100 days and still be fit and healthy. I knew that my best ideas didn't come from sitting in front of my laptop for fourteen hours solid with my bum going square. Determined, I promised myself I would complete ten hours of training every single week and still hit my audacious goal of $100k in 100 days. To ensure I kept to my promise to myself, I entered Ironman 70.3 in Taupo, New Zealand, which coincided with the end of this $100k 100-day sprint.

I committed to the plan and by the end of the 100 days, I'd exceeded the $100k mark *and* I had also managed to have an average of fourteen hours per week of training. I finished the Ironman 70.3 and I had an absolute blast doing it. This goes to show that you can prioritize your health and fitness and still be super successful in business.

Lots of experts talk about having a morning routine to set your body and mind up for the day. If you're anything like me, you get up, go for a wee, drink a glass of water, go outside, exercise, come back in and it's game on! It's time to feed myself, the cat and sort out my new baby. Then, I help my husband get out the door so that he can get to work. I enjoy my coffee and breakfast on the floor playing with my baby while sneaking quick peeks at Facebook and Instagram. I have a shower on turbo charge and dress while singing nursery rhymes and twerking. For some reason, my son thinks twerking is hilarious and laughs his gummy grin face off. Happy baby, happy life, right? By the time journaling and meditation comes around, it could be midday, or even the next day!

The whole get up, meditate for thirty minutes, drink water, do yoga, brush your hair backwards, write in your journal for thirty minutes, light a candle, and go through all your mantras, exercise, and have a sauna and all the other 'essentials' of a morning routine are clearly designed for someone who actually does nothing for the rest of the day. I don't know about you, but I'd need to get up at 3:00 in the morning to get all that shit done before the day actually started. Even when I didn't have a baby, I'd have to get up way too early to achieve such a routine. That means that I would be restricting my sleep, which is also one of the key important foundational blocks to having a healthy lifestyle.

So, I'm here to tell you, girl, that a morning routine doesn't have to be something you set an alarm for at ridiculous-o'clock; nor does it have to be restricted to the hours before midday. Your 'morning routine' can be pockets throughout the day that you can squeeze in to make sure that you are looking after your health.

The non-negotiables are, being able to get outside, every single day. Sweat. Connect with nature and feel the vibrational energy Mother Earth gives you. Note: that means you must leave your phone at home... or at least in your pocket, so you can be present.

Now, I know what it's like to live in -40 degrees Celsius; my sister-in-law lives in Banff National Park, Canada. We're so lucky to have her live there. When we visited it was—30ºC most of the time over Christmas, and I still managed to get outside and go for a run, a walk, a ski, or an ice skate. Well, the ice skating was more sweating than moving, as I was terrified! But the point I'm making is that I still managed to get out of the house, exercise, and connect to nature, to source, despite the temperature.

Even though it was bitterly cold, my face was about to burn off—and I had to put plastic bags in my running shoes, and inside my socks were heat warmers, so that my feet didn't freeze—I still got outside and did at least twenty minutes every day.

This is what I want you to focus on: getting outside for at least twenty minutes. You might be thinking but HOW? I am already up to my eyeballs in things to do. Or you could just not like physical activity. But moving can be as simple as running errands. Instead of jumping in the car, walk. I know, it sounds crazy; we are such a car society, but try walking. Walk down the road, you'll be surprised at how close things really are. Plus, you'll get your exercise in. #winwin

If you live in a rural area, this might not be so practical! I've lived on a farm before, so I know. Go for a walk around the farm, or go somewhere and meet people to go for a walk and have a chat. Don't make it a big deal that you 'have' to exercise each day. Reframe it to your time to shine. My Poppy used to say, 'Horses sweat, men perspire, and ladies glow.' So, get your glow on, lady!

This is where your greatest ideas, your greatest flow, will come out. I promise. It's all about connecting to source as we are primal human beings. Alex Charfen often Instagrams about his primal walk that he does every morning with his two daughters. He wears Vibram Five Fingers— or barefoot shoes—so that he can really be in touch with nature. It's fantastic if you can take your shoes off and actually have your feet and your toes in the grass. Not so good if it's -40 in snow... I wouldn't suggest taking your shoes off there!

Touch some trees as you walk past them and connect back to our natural source. Don't pluck the leaves off, though! How would you like it if someone plucked your hair out as they walked past you? Just feel them and breath in their filtered air. We are from nature; we have evolved through nature, and it is so important for us to be connected back to her.

I always thought being outside 'connecting to nature' every day was a bit woo, but it wasn't until I saw my husband have this connected-to-source experience first-hand, that I saw the power in the practise. My husband runs a very successful data analytics company, www.datagems.co.nz, where his team are the leading specialists in locational data for Australasia.

But it wasn't always like that. One Sunday, I said, "Come on, let's go for a walk,' and he really doesn't like walking; he finds it *really* boring. He's a typical boy, likes to go fast and out on the water; he's been a professional sailor before. But he came for a walk with me, knowing that it would keep me happy. We went and did quite a tough trail in the Waitakere Ranges in New Zealand, a beautiful area of native bush overlooking black sand beaches. We started at a waterfall and went right around the coast for about three hours, which is really stretching his usual threshold of twenty minutes with a takeaway coffee!

We alternated walking in silence, chatting a little bit, then again in silence, and really just being at one with nature. On the drive home—which is an hour or so back—he just blurted out, "Oh, my gosh, I absolutely hate what I'm doing." Like the waterfall we'd just hiked around, it all flowed out; he really let loose all the stuff that had been stuck in his head for so long.

The next week, he left his unfulfilling job and he decided to set up his own business; Datagems was born. He took on the principles of $100k in 100 days and he actually rocked straight through that six-figure mark way before I did. Side note: it was rather annoying, because we're quite competitive!

This shows you that just taking that time out and getting silent with yourself in nature, gives you the ability to be able to connect to what it is that is deep inside you. Because, you know what? You have all the answers deep inside you; you just need to give yourself the outside space and time to be able to find them. Often, you must be brave enough to let them come to the surface.

So, the main contributing factors to having a healthy body is being outside for at least twenty minutes a day. Start simply; start by walking around the block after dinner. This will help digest your food, and it will mean that you get outside. Drag your family or a friend out too, and spend some quality time together. Turn the TV off; you're not going to get any inspiration or ideas from television. I'll tell you that right now, unless you're watching YouTube TED Talks you're not getting any advantage by watching TV. You need to be quite disciplined to be able to only stick to TED too! Or simply try to get out in the morning, as it really refreshes you to see the sun come up, and sweat. Sweat is so important. (Sorry, 'glow', Grandad!)

Next, is your hydration. Most people do not hydrate enough. If you're not going for a wee every couple of hours, you are not hydrating enough. This needs to be good old plain water. The first thing that goes into your mouth when you wake up, must be water. Yes, before your coffee!

You sweat and lose so much water overnight that most people start the day off super dehydrated. This is how headaches and the chocolate cravings start later in the afternoon. If you drink two litres or more of distilled, purified water in the morning, then you are going to rock the afternoon without that chocolate bar. Alex Charfan puts it as, "daily hyper hydration."

I like to pop a drop of doTERRA lemon essential oil in to zing it up a bit and help things digest for the day. I will explain how you can use essential oils to manifest and bring that $100k to life in the next chapter. For now, know grab a BIG glass of water in the morning and guzzle, guzzle, guzzle, guzzle, guzzle.

Getting good sleep is the next thing to focus on in the list. Sleep—deep, restorative sleep—is extremely important to being able to function well the next day. Although it might seem tempting to stay up late just to get that last thing finished to meet the deadlines, it can be detrimental to your health; especially in today's world where everything has to be done right now, every second of the day. Unfortunately, putting sleep low on the list of priorities can lead to huge amounts of burnout putting you and your business at risk. I have even seen woman closing their businesses from burnout.

Adults need between seven and eight hours of sleep, every night. You may be able to function on less currently. You might also be thinking, "Oh, I'm one of those people that only needs to sleep five hours a night and I am fine, Penny." But I assure you, it will catch up with you in the end. One day, you'll be in the fog so deep that you won't realise what is happening. Because you can't see what is happening on the inside of your body right now. Restricted sleep has been found to be a major contributor to cell degenerative diseases and even worse, a shorter life span. Lack of sleep—and therefore, the ability to handle stress—is one of the contributing factors to why cancer is so prevalent in our generation.

Feel too stressed to drop everything and go to bed mid project? Your stress doesn't even have to be full blown 'arggghhh, I am about to explode'. It can be simple day-to-day pressure and noise. This builds up over time and becomes unmanageable when you haven't had enough sleep. It is harder to function and think rationally when you're in a sleep deprived fog. Ask any new mum what she did yesterday, and the blank stare you receive in response is a quick way for you to see what sleep deprivation does to you and your brain.

So, really, when you're putting your laptop down min project and going to bed on time or even earlier, you're actually saving your own life. It will decrease the stress, not increase it because the project is not complete. I want you to look at it like that and have all seriousness about it.

The other thing about having really good sleep is that you can deal with issues when they come up much more easily. Let's face it, when you're running a business, there will be issues. Sorry to burst the bubble, lovely. But when you've been getting great zzzs, you can deal with the refunds, tech issues, and online haters with a much more level head. You know yourself that if you are tired how difficult it is to focus on tasks, or how rushed you might be when you try to do things, and then you make mistakes. When you are fresh and revived, you feel amazing and are more accurate too.

Getting good sleep—like exercise and being outside—isn't done once a week. You can't run on six nights of five hours of sleep, and then have one big monster sleep on the weekend and think you're back on track. It doesn't work like that. You need to be focused on having sleep *every* night. Go to bed knowing that you need to have eight hours sleep. If you need to be up at six in the morning, then you need to go to bed before 10 so that you're asleep at 10PM. If you can sleep until eight, then you can go to bed at midnight. Know though the hours before midnight are worth more in your deep restorative sleep than they are after midnight. But as long as you are working back from your wake-up time to achieve eight hours then you're golden (another Kiwism for 'good'!).

I can hear the protesting now! "But, Penny, I don't think I can get everything done AND be in bed on time." Boo hoo to you. My husband protests EVERY night. I can assure you that you can get everything done and be in bed on time. Work out what you do at night that can be eliminated—TV, mucking around on social media, and Netflix are BIG time suckers. These time wasters are not helping you move your business forward. Sleep—deep, restorative sleep—will.

So, switch off the screens, grab a good book (like this one) and go old skool; read paper pages before bed. Wind down, do some gentle stretching, meditate, or lie there and just run through all the things you're grateful for. Then, enjoy lovely deep sleep.

The reason why so many practices such as mediation, journaling, yoga, and colouring in have come into fruition with huge followings in the past three years, is because of the fact that it actually takes time to slow down. No-one likes to slow down. But if you don't do it yourself, your body will do it for you.

Sleep is going to give you rest, brain development, restorative relaxation, and keep your cortisol levels down so that you don't put on weight, especially around your stomach area. Bonus! Not having a muffin top means that you're going to feel whole lot better about yourself when you pull on your skinny jeans too.

Essentially, sleep is key. If you're not able to get out, meditate, do yoga, write in a journal, drink all your water, or go outside and exercise—the fastest way for you to look after yourself is to get that extra hour sleep a night.

If you can get those three things right, then all the rest is added bonus. Green smoothies, supplements, writing in your journal, meditating, yoga—any kind of stillness activities—are all added bonuses on top of these three core principles.

Remember: the main thing is this needs to be a daily routine. It's not something you do once a week and think, "I've ticked the box, yay. I'm gonna be able to be a successful millionaire in my business." These are daily habits that need to happen to be able to make sure that you—the most important person in your business—is functioning at 100% capacity every day. Not just on Monday when you feel refreshed after the weekend and you're totally fading by Friday. But this absolutely needs to happen every day of the week. Set it as a routine and you will be well into your 70s and 80s still with a very successful business and being the head of it, healthy and strong.

GET MOMENTUM KEY POINTS

1. Get outside for some sort of exercise that makes you sweat for 20 minutes a day to clear your head and connect to source.
2. The first thing to do (after your morning wee) is drink a HUGE glass of water.
3. Eight hours sleep a night; your day starts the night before, so get to bed 8 hours before you need to get up.

Chapter 6:

Your Senses and Your Subconscious are Best Buds

When it comes to your senses —sight, smell, sound, taste, and touch—you may be really in tune with the first sight and how that forms images in your subconscious. We all see what we want and make decisions on what we can see. For example, we eat with our eyes first! But I was unaware of how impactful the other four senses are on our subconscious mind, until I did an NLP exercise with Louise Blakely.

Take a quick minute is to sit there, clear your mind, put down this book (once you've read what to do), and think about a lemon. I want you to think about how sweet or sour a lemon can be. Think about the colour of the outside of the lemon and it's firmness. Think about how your face looks when you suck on a lemon or even just bite through the waxy outside into the soft juicy centre. Think about the flavour that comes out.

Take a big breath...

How are you feeling?

If you're anything like me, you'll be wincing your face up, and your mouth will be salivating. There'll be quite a lot of saliva in your mouth right now. This is your senses reacting to a previous experience in your subconscious. You know that a lemon is generally very sour, and it will feel really, really yucky biting into a lemon, so your brain is giving you the reaction just at the thought of it.

From this easy example, you can see just how much your senses react to what is in your subconscious. I was shocked to realise this.

When I was going back through how I achieved the $100k in 100 days, I had a strategy. Sure, there was lots of mindset work, but I went really deep on what ALL the details were so that I could share 100% open book exactly with you how I cracked $100k in 100 days.

One of the interesting factors in my 100-day sprint was a very dear friend of mine, Lynne Taggart. Lynne sent me two sample essential oils and she said, "These are gonna blow your mind. Take a drop of each and put them onto the soles of your feet before you sit down to work or be creative, and especially before your sales calls." I wanted to give everything a shot to be able to make this $100k in 100 days, and so I thought 'why not?'.

Now I'm usually very sceptical about woo woo things like this and think, 'Oh, I don't really see how that could make much difference'. But it made a massive difference, and looking back on my time where I cracked that first $100k in 100 days, it was one of the key contributing factors to heightening my senses. Which in turn re-programmed my subconscious; all from the soles of my feet. How cool is that?

So, what was in the brew I hear you screaming?

Wild Orange was one of them, the other was Lemon. Both were doTERRA Essential Oils which are 100% pure oil, meaning you're not putting any other chemicals into your body and giving you a toxin-free sensation.

It was once I started rubbing these on my feet that I actually saw some really solid breakthroughs in the number of potential clients taking notice of what I was putting out into the environment. The oils helped me get my message really nice and clear. When I sat down to journal and think through what it was that I wanted to say to people, the oils worked with my senses to move my subconscious into a state to bring out the clarity I needed; to really get into the vibration to have all the ideas and creativity flow out. No more writers block and stuckness.

Essential oils work with your neurovascular system, the sole of your foot being the fastest absorption area to apply to. One drop rubbed in takes 22 seconds for molecules to be found in the brain, 2 minutes they can be found in the bloodstream and 20 minutes they can be found in every cell in your body.

Pure essential oils facilitate not only physical but emotional and spiritual healing. There are five stages of healing from an oil.

1. Healing in the physical body
2. Healing the heart
3. Releasing limiting beliefs
4. Spiritual awareness and connection
5. Fulfilment of our life's purpose.

Points 3, 4, and 5 were where I saw the biggest break throughs. Being able to be free to really go for my big dream and release the limiting beliefs. All by rubbing some oil on my feet. It almost felt like I was cheating!

You, too, can have this through using the five following oils that I suggest every savvy biz chick should have.

Lemon—the oil of clarity and focus. Have you had times when you can't concentrate or something feels so hard? Maybe setting up a funnel and coping with the tech side? Or was it trying to work out just what to do next and then the steps it will take? A few drops of lemon rubbed in your hands and soles of your feet with do the trick to bring you the clarity and concentration you desire.

Lavender—the oil for reducing anxieties around manifesting. Used for communication and freeing you from the 'I shoulds' to knowing what you want and being able to be emotionally honest with yourself. It stops those racing thoughts that keep you stuck and not taking action—like the Live video you said you would do or the email you said you'd send out.

Peppermint—to give you energy to get through the day and keep being persistent and consistent. Rub a drop into the top of mouth for a super energy blast. Much more zing than a coffee or afternoon chocolate fix.

Frankincense—the oil of truth. This oil is used for all emotions really—it's the bomb! Helps to keep you loved and protected, especially when trying new things like we do every day in our businesses. It will help release the darkness out to let in new light and ideas. I love this one in the diffuser.

Wild Orange—my all-time fav and what I used the most in my $100k in 100 days challenge. The oil of Abundance. Place a few drops on the soles of feet before entering your workspace and see the magic unfold.

If these tickle your fancy, then jump onto my website for these oils and any other gems I am experimenting with at www.pennyelliott.com/oils

GET MOMENTUM KEY POINTS

1. Essential oils are actually effective, not woo woo.
2. Your senses and your subconscious are best buds. Your thoughts react to your senses, so use your senses wisely.
3. Use oils to reach your goals. Apply oils that stir up the right thoughts and feelings to put you in the right space to achieve.

CHAPTER 7:

Writing Your Way to Manifesting $100k in 100 Days

There are many examples out there where people have written their way to manifesting their dreams and desires. One world-famous, and well-noted individual who did this is Jim Carrey who wrote himself a $10 million-dollar check when he was on Struggle Street. He put it in his wallet, having faith that he would be able to bank it one day. He then landed the role in Dumb and Dumber and found out he would get paid—wait for it: $10 million dollars.

I found this fascinating, yet the sceptic in me thought rather fluky. But so many more examples can be found, that I just had to dive in and give it a try. Low and behold, the power of writing out my manifestations was one of the powerful ways I went about cracking the $100k in 100 days. In fact you're 42% more likely to hit your goals when you physically write them down.

I bought myself a KikkiK journal, the 365-journal where you write a page a day, and I committed to myself to journaling every single day. (Side Note – Kikki K is gorgeous

Scandinavian stationery that is an obsession of mine! Started and owned by Kristina Karlsson who was a young girl passionate about stationary, but broke, the company now has 102 stores worldwide! Do what you're passionate about!)

I like to keep several diaries; one which is all about my list of to-does, what I want to achieve, my goals. Another for my training, and another for my travels. I've always done that and it stemmed from my great, amazing, wonderful grandmother, Jean Margaret Comins, whom I used to call Grammy. She kept a diary for every single day of her life and I'm very fortunate to be able to have those diaries now, and look back at them. I get to look through the eyes of how she saw the world each day.

She kept a journal of her travels to London, going back to see her family and she had her 36th birthday in Burgon. Side note: I actually happened to be in Burgon on the same that day that she was there about thirty years later, which was very, very special.

I digress.

Grammy always told me to keep a diary because as time goes on, you forget the little bits and bobs that you saw, thought, or did. So, I always kept a travel journal, a sports journal, AND a business journal. Even though everything's digitised now, I love to be able to physically write down how I felt after each session or be able to actually see my thoughts down there on paper.

But it's different when you want to manifest the future in your writing instead of documenting what has happened.

We're talking about how to manifest your future dreams and desires through writing, not documenting what you saw and did for the day. On my journey to $100k in 100 days, I had this 365 KikkiK journal to write for manifestation. In it I didn't write, "Today I played with the cat, took her for a walk, and wrote an email to my list." I didn't also write, "Tomorrow I'm going to do this, this, and this."

The key to changing your world or your subconscious is to write it as if you've already achieved it. This is a very different writing style, so I want to share with you some extracts from my journal and just how they came true.

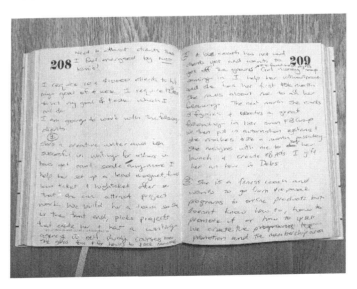

In the early days of the $100k in 100 days challenge, I was very sceptical about whether I would actually make it. It seemed like such an audacious goal! Who was I to achieve this? Yet, in these pages you can see that I have actually written, "I will get to $100k. I'm not sure how, but it is going to happen."

As the days ticked over, I could see my audaciousness coming to fruition. What I was writing was coming true. This fuelled me and my writing became even more positive, because I could see it already happening.

You might find this style a bit hard to grasp at first and feel fake writing down your big goal as if it's already happened. So, another way to manifest through writing is by writing a letter to yourself. For example; "Dear future self, I need this person and this person to move my business forward to the next step. I know that this will happen and love working with this person. They are exactly the help I need and I am loving seeing the progress we are making. How are you doing? Love Penny."

I've done this exact exercise while I was sitting in the crowd at Funnel Hacking Live, the annual Click Funnels conference. Side note: AMAZING conference where we got to spend time with Tony Robbins!

While being totally pumped in the audience about the business I was going to build to get my 2 Comma Club Award, I wrote that I needed to get myself a funnel builder, a designer, and a social media person to be able to grow my platforms.

Although I wrote that, I didn't write it as a to-do list but as
something that I wanted to manifest.

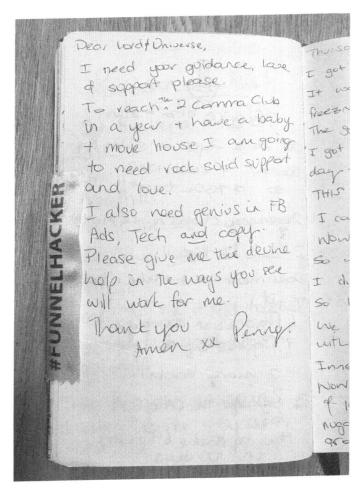

I then left it to the Universe. I went hiking the week after I
got back to New Zealand, and thought nothing more of my
request. Literally that following week, I had all three people

pop up and work with me. Because I already had my ideal in my subconscious from writing it down. I then went about some inspired action and popped a comment in the ClickFunnels group on a post about someone who was writing about a funnel.

The guy who responded happened to be Australasia's best funnel builder and he's gone on to be absolutely amazing worldwide. Russell Brunson totally recommends him and is now part of Alex Charfen's and Rachel Pederson's team. Chris Benetti is amazing. I totally manifested our paths crossing through writing out my intentions in my journal.

As you can see, what you want and desire in the world can be manifested through your journaling. Now, as I alluded to, this is not a to-do list. This is not an I've done list and it's not an account of what you've done throughout the day. This is what you want to achieve and written in a tense as if you've already achieved what you require.

These are some fantastic written manifesting tools that I was given to be able to manifest my $100k in 100 days.

The first tool is to journal daily on your big dream goals.

I want you to use these journal prompts to manifest your big dreams and goals, which you've already decided and declared to yourself and your family and friends by now.

- If I could have anything happen today, it would be…

- I have already achieved (write out your big goal as it is already done).
- My ideal day is…
- Money flows easily to me via…

Note: If you've skipped ahead just to this bit, then go back to beginning and set your big dream goal! I know those kinds of people. They're out there. I see you trying to take short cuts! Ha. Busted!

It is now time to use these prompts to manifest your dream goals. Write about them every day. If you find it hard to get journaling without just writing out a to do list—cos I know I used to—I have popped a huge list of journal prompts in the free workbook with this book at www.pennyelliott.com/book.

The next tool is to write down the next five clients you want. Again, use the workbook to save the margins of this book!

Now, this doesn't have to be like, "Oh. I want a client, and she's gonna pay me X amount of money, and I'm gonna feel great." This is getting into the emotional side of what you want so you can really feel it and change the wiring in your subconscious. Get in the right vibe!

To do this, you need to get into what they look like. Where do they come from? I want you to describe what she looks like, what she wears, what problems she has that you can solve. Is she like you? Do you see her? What's her name and what is she coming to you for? I also want you to write down what results she's achieved with you, what you both worked through, and the feeling when the outcome was delivered.

How did you feel with her results? How did it make you react? How has it changed your life? I want you to write them all down in the present tense as an, "I have. I am. This is."

This will help you create the right vibe and the right feeling within you, much like the emotional freedom technique we spoke of in an earlier chapter. Knowing what your future ideal clients look and feel like will help you bring your aura around you into a world of this-is-happening-no-matter-what.

When you do this, your brain starts to think that 'this is happening', then it will actually seek out those things to make it true in your world. A good example of this is when you start looking at buying a new car.

I really want an Audi S3. I had one in the UK and I'd really like one now that I live back in New Zealand. As soon as I start looking at Audis in the dealership, cutting the pictures out, writing about my dream Audi, I see them everywhere. I dive deep into how I'm driving it, how it feels, and what I feel like driving it. I feel how I take off from the lights, because I'm a little bit of a girl racer at heart, and how my wee boy Joshua looks in the back of it in his car seat. I see how I can fit his mates in, and their soccer balls that are in the boot, the bikes on the bike rack on the back...

I really, really get into the nitty gritty of the details and emotion. I can even smell the fresh leather of the seats. Once I have done this exercise, I now see an Audi everywhere I look. I'm like, "There's my Audi. There's another Audi, there's another Audi."

But, there's not more Audis on the road, right? It's just that I'm bringing it from the subconscious into my conscious. So, I'm noticing those cars more than when it was just a wish to own one.

You must be exactly the same with any item. Whatever that you want to purchase—say it's a pink jumper—all of the sudden you see everyone wearing that pink sweater or everyone has a Mont Blanc pen all of a sudden.

It's not that Mont Blanc pens have gone on special, because they never do; it's more the fact that you are starting to bring this pen into your aura. This is what we want you to do in your business goals.

By writing about the five ideal clients with whom you want to work as if you already have them, you will bring these people into existence. Go for it!

The next writing manifesting tool is to pretend you're being interviewed by Oprah. You can either do a voice recording or you can write it down. I want you to fast forward yourself to the place where you've made the $100k in 100 days and someone like Oprah—or your favourite TV show host—is going to interview you and ask what the process was for getting to the $100k in 100 days.

I want you to be able to articulate exactly how you did it, how you felt in that break through moment. Speak about how the opportunities all suddenly opened up for you. How you're even greater now that you've hit the six-figure mark. Really dig into your feelings. Feelings, as you know now, are important, because this is helps bring things to life in your subconscious.

I then want you to put away the interview for 24 hours. The next day come back to it. Either listen or reread what you said. You'll be very excited to actually think, "Wow. This has actually happened." It's amazing how it really does feel like it's already done in your world.

The last important part of writing your way to manifesting $100k in 100 is through a daily practice of gratitude. When you show gratitude, it tells the Universe that you've really appreciated what it has delivered to you *and* you'd like more of it. Writing it down is especially powerful.

The flip side of that is when you complain about stuff—the crap that goes wrong—then the Universe is like, "Well, she's talking a lot about that, lets deliver more of that to her." Your brain is actually manifesting and hard wiring more crap.

It's much like when we spoke about the previous chapter about the nasty girl inside of you. We want to get rid of that.

82

That's the same with your focus on bad things in your life. A really excellent way of focusing on the pure good and rewiring your thinking is to write down what you're grateful for at the end of each day.

I recommend you choose six things that you're grateful for each night and write those down. Now, they might be things that you *want* to be grateful about as well as the things that *are already* in your life. For example, you might actually bring in a new car so you'd write, "I'm grateful for my new car."

Now, you might be driving a tiny twenty-year-old car, but you're grateful for that new car coming into your world. That Audi S3. Right? You're grateful for it already!

Other things to be grateful for is your health, you family, a dry home, running water, the sun shining. It doesn't have to be BIG, flashy things. Never forget that. After the previous chapter you now understand how important health is to you, and your business, and your family. Because, without it you ain't got any of them, so show your gratitude daily.

Daily gratitude becomes a habit and then becomes a really beautiful documentation to go back and look on. It is wonderful to see the things you were grateful for a year ago and how they've actually manifested and come true in your life.

Much like Jim Carrey writing the ten-million-dollar check to himself; much like me writing down that I wanted to create

$100k in 100 days and actually having a giggle to myself thinking, "This is ludicrous. I've never made this amount of money before in such a short period." You actually can look back in your journal and say, "Wow. This is amazing." Where, if it was just listing your gratitude in your head, you can't actually go back and peek at them. It doesn't have that same positive feedback loop for your brain to create more and more opportunities.

I must touch on the importance of using a pen and paper for this manifestation process too. A lot of people just don't write anymore, as we're moving everything onto a screen. It's not even a keyboard anymore, it's all on glass.

Interestingly enough, huge tech companies are reverting back to handwriting as neurological pathways are set in the brain from the actual drawing of the letter. It also requires us to slow down and by doing this, we express in a much deeper way than when we strike a key. Research has shown that the actual movement of your hand from your brain out onto a piece of paper, helps ease the idea out of your head. It's much more therapeutic and also ingrains and retrains the neurologic pathways in your brain more than doing it on your phone or laptop.

You might be thinking, "Okay, well I can just type this out; it's so much quicker, and I can do it on my phone while I'm walking around." But I really would like you to go and get yourself a beautiful journal and see how much more in depth you go with your thoughts, and therefore your manifestation.

On your phone, it's just seen as another App. Another glass, tech thing. It's not actually flowing from deep within and out of you, and we really want it to float out of you to rewire your brain to be thinking like the woman who has created $100k in 100 days.

I'm a self-pronounced stationary geek; I love all the KikkiK stuff. I also love Franks Stationary, because with every journal that you buy, they provide one for a child, which I think is fantastic to get kids off glass and expressing themselves. I love social entrepreneurs that give back to the world too.

While you're at it get a beautiful pen. I absolutely adore my Mont Blanc. A very special person gave it to me and I cling to it like there's no tomorrow. Each time I write with it, I feel posh and luxurious. This higher vibration helps the manifestations to come out of my head, process, and back in and into reality faster.

Still feeling a bit stuck? Pop over to www.pennyelliott.com/book to download my latest journal prompts to get the juices flowing so that you can really manifest those dreams and desires that we've laid out in this section.

Note, if you've been naughty and skipped that chapter, because you don't actually like writing, go back and read it! I see you! Because it is one of the **most** important chapters of this whole, entire book—if not the most important chapter.

GET MOMENTUM KEY POINTS

1. Writing your gratitude journal will open neural pathways to align with your goals. Going back to your gratitude journal in time will tell a beautiful story of manifestation.

2. Visualisation is a powerful way to create the world you want to experience. Write it out in full colour. Use a pen and paper to slow down the process so you get really deep inner thoughts out and therefore the best manifestations.

I really hope that you've enjoyed the Woo side of business. It is now time to head on over to the strategy side: The Doo!

There is no point in trying to manifest all your big dreams and goals by spending all your time journaling, meditating, getting outside, doing exercise, hyper hydrating, and surrounding yourself with the right type of people if you're not actually doing any action.

I really hate to say it, but if you sit around doing a whole lot of the Woo and none of the Doo, then it doesn't matter how hard you try and manifest something —it ain't gonna happen until you do the doo, sista!

Business is fifty percent strategy and fifty percent mindset. We worked on the mindset and now it's time to hit the strategy. See you in Section Two.

Section 2:

Strategy—The Doo

So, now that you've got a confident mindset—you're manifesting like a mofo, using the Universal vibe, mastered meridian energy lines through EFT, know exactly your dream goals, are surrounding yourself with the people to make it happen, and have a super healthy body—it is time for the business strategy: the Doo. It is really important that we've laid down those foundational pieces as you now have fantastic habits to support the strategy.

It is now really important to do the action—inspired action, baby!

With this confident, unstoppable mindset, you'll be able to take inspired action. Now, this is different from just any old action... Action is what you used to do at your nine-to-five when you sat down and you ground out what you needed to do. Sure, that's action.

But inspired action comes from the vibration that you're putting out to the Universe. So, now that you have the Woo practices in motion, amazing ideas will start to come through to you—creative thought or divine alignment that make you think 'boom, I've got this! I know what I need to do!'

It's now time to take that lightning bolt thought and put it in to inspired action. Therefore, this section is called the Doo. There's no point in having any woo without any doo. Because you need to actually do the Doo to move your business forward.

I am going to be the bearer of very bad news. If you want to sit round journaling, doing yoga, and meditating about your dreams and goals and you don't actually want to get off your ass and do the doo, then those dreams are never gonna come to you. Plain and simple: you're never going to win Lotto if you don't go and buy a lotto ticket every single week until you win it, right?

In this section, we're going to explore exactly what to do so you can manifest your dreams and desires and make $100k in 100 days, using the exact steps I did.

CHAPTER 8:

No More Guessing or Assuming. Get Gritty with Your Ideal Client.

There's a saying that assumption is the mother of all fuck ups and it's so true. As soon as you start assuming you know what someone's thinking or what someone wants without asking for clarity, it will always end up not being the right thing for them. Or worse still, you might be thinking they want something and they actually don't at all.

So, the very first thing that you need to do when you are launching any new product, service, business, or idea is to get really gritty with who your ideal client is and what they really want right now—not what you think they need, but what they want - right now.

For example, if you are a dietitian or a nutritionist and you want to help people lose weight, you know damn well that they need to give up coffee because it's a stimulant. It raises your cortisol levels and causes a slump later in the afternoon that leads to hitting up the vending machine for non-nutritious snacks —that's a brief, non-scientific way of describing what coffee can do for some people. In other words, removing coffee means that it removes the high at the beginning of the day. It then removes the desire for the high in the afternoon, which is usually achieved with a chocolatey, sugary treat. Thus, reducing your butt.

However, if you went out and advertised 'quit coffee and lose weight', you probably wouldn't get very many people to sign up because coffee is one of the most addictive substances on the planet, right after alcohol and even better: it's legal to have! Coffee is legal for any age, whereas alcohol is restricted to 18 plus. So, telling people that they have to quit the thing they love the most right out of the gate isn't the best way of charming people. It's giving them what they need, not what they want.

What you do need to do is speak to your client about where they're at *right now*. It's about losing weight and letting go of that sugary slump in the afternoon. Then, once you've brought them in and they trust and like you more, you can start talking about removing coffee and they will believe you about the effect it has on their body. They won't see ditching their beloved coffee as such a huge loss and try to cut it out. If you started off with the hard-hitting thing that you know that they need right from the beginning, they'd be like 'Piss off! There is no way I am going to give up my morning coffee. Surely, there's some other way.' They will simply go with someone else.

Now, if you're anything like me, research is booorrring and you really do not want to get into it; you'd rather get to the fun stuff of creating. I thought 'I want to create this. I'm really good at this and I'm going to sell it. I can sell anything on the planet.'

But I was oh-so wrong!

I want to tell you a little story about that arrogant, ego-based person I used to be.

I was approached by Gabby Bernstein's team to be one of her affiliates to sell her course *Spirit Junkie*, a couple of years ago. I was so excited that I had been asked, because here I thought I was this little person sitting in New Zealand, unnoticed by many people, and still growing my reach. And here was a giant in our coaching industry, an amazing woman who had her team reach out to me, and asked if I wanted to sell her only product that she sells each year. Wow!

There was a group of only two-hundred of us from the whole entire world and more than fifty-thousand coaches (and growing) to pick from. I thought "Wow, this is an honour. I'm so excited to sell *Spirit Junkie* and be part of the movement!"

Now, part of selling *Spirit Junkie* is that each affiliate gets to package something with the course to sweeten the deal so that people will want to jump in and buy *Spirit Junkie* through you and then they get all of these bonuses for free. I thought, easy,

I'm going to do *a Super Soulful Selling Live* course. I'm going to create something around how to sell from your soul and not sound so cheesy.

I felt confident that my audience wanted to not sound so cheesy when they were selling. I went ahead and I created all the modules, the sales page, and all the bonuses. I then did four free training webinars and a full week's Open Cart email series. It included all the bells and whistles for a whole month selling *Super Soulful Selling* course with *Spirit Junkie*.

The result of all that creation and selling?

I sold two people into that course, and one of them decided that she didn't want to continue with the course before the calls even started! I share this openly because this does happen, and it is part of business. It's not a reflection on you; it's just a reflection on their circumstances. Refunds are a percentage of your business and you should always factor them in.

So, that left me with one person for over eight weeks of creation and effort. That one client went through the course and absolutely loved it.

Was it worth my time in Woo? Absolutely. I was to be able to be of service to her and helped her gain clarity and clients.

Was it worth my time in a business Doo? Not at all! There is no way eight weeks' worth of creating and selling and then a seven-week course was worth doing for one student. I never broke even, let alone made any profit.

Now, it is glaringly obvious that I had not done my market research beforehand. Isn't hindsight a bitch? Not once had I asked my community where they were at right now, what they needed to hear or feel; what process they wanted to go through, and where they were, or what would help them take the next step. I had no idea. I knew I was good at sales. I knew I wanted to sell the *Spirit Junkie* course and needed an affiliate bonus to attach to it. I knew that people would gain some great traction with the *Spirit Junkie* course if they knew how to sell, too. But I didn't put any consideration into what my audience actually wanted.

Now, if I had done the research and taken an extra week out of the eight weeks of promotion to really get gritty with what my audience wanted, and grow that audience, and grow and build something that matched what they wanted, my course would have sold like hotcakes.

My gorgeous friend, Lynne Taggart, did. She took a lot of time doing research and asking lots of questions. She then built a package around her community's responses and the *Spirit Junkies* course. When the open cart came, people were gagging to get in—she sold twenty people in and made huge changes in her clients lives.

So, the lesson here is to spend time in research mode and get really gritty with your ideal clients. How do you do that? I'll show you. By using the questions found in the accompanying workbook at www.pennyelliott.com/book you can easily survey your community, your list, or someone else's Facebook group. Make sure that you write down the answers so you can see the patterns emerging. Build your offer from here up. More on how to do this in the next chapter.

GET MOMENTUM KEY POINTS

1. Don't assume you know what your customers want. Get gritty – ASK them!
2. Speak to them at the level they're at right now – not where you want them to be.
3. Look for emerging patterns and build your service or product around that.

CHAPTER 9:

Create What They Want, Not What You Think They Need.

As I alluded to in the previous chapter, the intersection of a hotcake product that flies off the shelf happens when you find something that you're good at and it is something that people want.

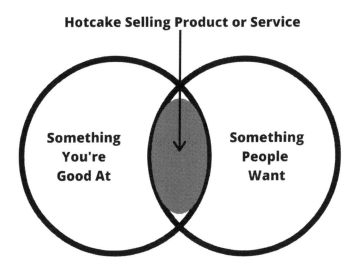

To illustrate this, I want to tell you a wee story about when I used to work at Lindt Chocolate. (Ghirardelli in America). I worked there for over three years and absolutely loved every minute of it, including all the free chocolate. When I first started, we were told that we had to try every single chocolate so that we knew exactly what we were selling. Needless to say, in the first two months, my chocolate intake skyrocketed and so did my weight! I was less than impressed, and I had to curb it back after a month or so. Yes, once you do have access to unlimited chocolate supply, you do actually cut back in the end, and settle for probably a higher equilibrium than you're used to—but you don't eat it ceaselessly like you think you would.

Let's start the story I'm here to tell you about. When I worked at Lindt, we had a huge market research team, as it is a multi-million-dollar business in the UK, America, and Europe. The European population's palate is much more refined than it is in the UK—no offense, UK readers, but it is a fact. Research has shown that that's not just an opinion, but in Europe, the consumption habits of chocolate are quite different. They'll have one slice of chocolate after a meal and really savour it. In contrast, in the UK, they've been brought up on Cadbury, and therefore the English like to have thicker chocolate—that real chomp bite—and actually chew on the chocolate. English eat chocolate by the block full and at any time of the day.

So, when it came to selling Lindt in the UK against their competitor Cadbury, there was a real difference between consumption habits. It was hard for the European chocolatiers to understand that actually the UK market doesn't like these thin squares that had a really good snap to it. They really enjoyed a lumpier confectionary—like Cadbury or the one that has a centre in them. They look like little pillows every time you snap off a block of chocolate—or a row, if you're really in a different league.

What this shows is that there definitely was a skill to making the chocolate for people's wants. Even a multi-million-dollar chocolate industry can show you that they needed to learn the intersection of what they were good at—which was making amazing chocolate—and what the consumers wanted, country-dependent shapes, instead of just producing what they thought the market needed. Europeans eat chocolate in a more refined way. They enjoy one or two squares a night with their meal, which would obviously reduce obesity rate and sugar consumption, while combatting a deluge of health benefits.

However, the UK consumer wanted a pillow chocolate. As soon as Lindt Europe decided to create these pillow chocolates for the UK market, we saw sales rocket in this area and started to become competitive with the Cadbury giant. They found the magic connection between what they're good at and what consumers wanted.

Another really good example is easily seen when you go to the supermarket. You buy what you want, especially if it's a treat and not necessarily what you need. And so, they have now dedicated a whole aisle to potato crisps, another whole aisle to sweets, candy or lollies (as we call them here in New Zealand) and chocolates, and another whole aisle to frozen goods, such as desserts and pizza—all of which we do not need. But they're all things we *want*.

Now, before you take off for a choccy break, let's think about your business: where you're going and the dreams and goals that you've picked out. Are you creating something that you're good at, that you're your own mini expert at, and something that your customers *want*? Remembering the real difference between want and need.

Use the accompanying workbook found at www.pennyelliott.com/book and fill in the spheres of what you're good at and what your ideal client wants. This illustrative exercise can make it so easy to see the intersection point.

Now, it is really hard to step out of your own ego and think "What do people want?" So, when people want to lose weight, for example, people don't necessarily want to give up all the things that they love (for example coffee or chocolate). What they do want, firstly—always— , is a quick fix and secondly, they always want to feel good about themselves. They need to reduce calories and get more active. But what they want is to be able to go to the beach and not have to wear a t-shirt over their bikini because they're so embarrassed of their bodies.

Maybe they want to be able to fit into all their clothes again after having a baby. Maybe they want to look into their wardrobe and not feel so scared about the fact that they can't fit into any of the clothes that used to fit.

So, really think about what your customers *want*. Remember the golden rule: People buy only what they want, not what they need.

Make sure you know exactly what you're good at. It may be very difficult for you if you feel like "Well, I know a little bit about this, or a little bit about that, but I'm not really good at anything."

I want you to think really widely and broadly. You might not have direct experience and a certification or a degree, but you may have had the weight loss journey of losing seventy pounds and so, you have the real-life experience that no degree can give you. Or you may have had four children and now you have a really banging body because you have really worked on it, and you know a system that works for mums with small kids who wish to get their bodies back again. This is so much more helpful to a struggling mum than a personal trainer who has all the education but no children themselves, right?

You might know exactly the best recipe for making cakes that last more than one day. Or you might know the exact way to tidy up something to give you much more space in your life. So, you don't need to have a degree—you don't need to be Marie Kondo and have an absolute degree in tidying up—to be able to help someone in a messy need. There is a great saying that the fourth grader looks like a king or queen to the third grader. Be the fourth grader, not the principal of the school; that's all you need to do.

You don't have to be the be-all and end-all and know absolutely everything in a subject to be ahead of someone else, even if it's just half that step. People will look up to you. So, when you're writing your list of things that you're good at on your sphere, don't be harsh on yourself. Go back to the Woo work on conscious language. If you really can't be nice to yourself, think about what your friend would write down and write it from your their perspective. That often helps us get the juices out of exactly what we're good at.

GET MOMENTUM KEY POINTS

1. What are you really good at?
2. What is it your ideal client wants? (Note: this is not necessarily what you have to offer) You need to fine-tune your offer to meet their exact need, not what they want.
3. Failure is inevitable. Learn from it! Move on and don't beat yourself up.

CHAPTER 10:

People buy what they want to move from pain to pleasure.

We've covered the sphere intersection of a hot product that sells combining what you're good at and what your tribe wants in the last chapter. Now, we want to talk about how your community becomes motivated to buy your hot product.

Now, let's look back at the Lindt Chocolate example again. Usually, you're motivated to get off the couch and go down the road and buy the chocolate because of the cues in your head or the desire to have something sweet. Yet, often it's to feel love, and we don't even realise that the chocolate has hidden endorphins that release the same feelings as being in love does. That is your true motivation; to move from the painful place of feeling lonely on the couch to the pleasurable feeling of love—not actually the chocolate itself.

Another great example is when you go to the dentist. Let's be honest, most people only ever go to the dentist when they're in pain—except for the very diligent few who go every six months for hygiene check-ups. Who are these people?!

When you're in the dentist's chair, she doesn't sit there and go, "Oh, so how does it feel? Well, maybe we can book you in next week or the week after." Nope, what does she do? She gets that metal handled hook and scrapes all around your teeth. It hurts like hell. Then she goes, "Right, let's see which one it is. Does this hurt?" She proceeds to tap with the handle end of the hook onto your tooth, and keeps tapping along like she's knocking on your front door, until she finds the one that makes you let out a ginormous yelp. Then she says, "Right, that one's the problem. We need to give you a filling or a root canal."

You don't even ask how much it is going to be, because you're still reeling from the pain of the metal handle tapping your sore tooth. The only thing you can think of is, "Do whatever it takes but make it stop hurting!"

Once the filling is done, the only pain you have left is at the front desk when you have to pay. Yet, this pain is minimal, because you no longer have that searing pain in your jaw. You've moved from pain to pleasure. You can now carry on your day without gripping your jaw when you eat something cold or hard. The money was not an objection that crossed your mind.

This is a very graphical explanation of how you want your customers to buy from you. You want to be able to talk to them about their pain points, and then show them what you're able to do for them—the transformation to a place of pleasure.

People don't buy on the fact that you can give them ten yoga classes for $100. They buy on the transformation. They buy the fact that they can come to you with a sore back, low energy, and after ten classes—or on the way through ten classes—they're going to raise their energy levels. Their backs won't hurt nearly as much, and they're going to really move into this new place of pleasure, a new vibration.

It's the transformation that people really want to buy. So, you need to know what their pain points are and what the pleasure is they're moving towards that you provide. This was a really important revolution in my $100k in 100 days journey.

Can you see how the transformation comes from knowing how you need to dig into their pain, and then show them that bright future? Yet so many times when I work with clients, they really don't want to dig into the pain and they just want to talk about the rosiness. They feel mean or nasty highlighting the fact that their ideal client's life sucks at the moment and they need to do something about it.

However this is where you really need to put your people pleasing ego aside, and put on your service hat on to be serving to that person. I've had some amazing coaches in the past, and one of them shared the recording of her sales call with a lady. In the teaching she said, "I'm very glad that I finally got her to get her commit to pay for coaching, because otherwise I was just letting her off the hook."

When I listened to the replay of the call, she was very determined that this woman should come and have coaching with her. I thought 'wow that was pretty forward of her'. Yet, it turned out to be the best thing that this woman had ever done. By being lead to pay for coaching she really get out of her own way which was keeping her small. She went on to grow an amazing business that helped her to have economic independence and treat her family to all sorts of nice experiences. This would not have happened if my coach was too afraid to drill in to her pain points.

Now, if you are not highlighting your ideal client's pain, and helping them transform, then you're just leaving people out there high and dry. Say you have the cure for cancer, would you sit around at home and hold on to it? No! You'd get it out there to everyone. You would have to talk to the people who have cancer, and tell them, "Hey, you've got cancer which, left untreated, might just kill you. Yet, here's the cure I've made for you."

You wouldn't be thinking 'Oooh, not sure if I want to mention that they might die from cancer'! You'd be screaming it from the rooftops that you have the cure—no more pain, no more sickness, and the possibility of seeing your family and living a full life.

See the difference? See how you're not hurting them, you're being in service to them?

This is exactly what you're doing with your product or service. By staying at home, not putting yourself out there, and not talking to people's pain, you're just being light and fluffy. You're not motivating people to get off their butts and actually take action. To make a better life for themselves.

For example; if you want to help people build their businesses, then you need to be able to show them that they're in a rut right now; by coming to you to help them grow their businesses, you will be able to ensure that they will have the life that they dream of. You might be helping people with their social media. At the moment they might be posting one or two times a day yet not getting any traction, not really moving forward. By working with you, they will be able to ensure that they're not wasting their time, posting the right content and they are actually getting the traction that they desire from the social media.

When you're starting your sales pages or any of your sales copy and you feel sleezy or worried that you'll make people cringe, remember it's actually helping them transform. So, let's change that word from sleazy to "transform". I don't want you to be afraid about highlighting their pain. Maybe you don't know what their pain points are right now. This comes from getting gritty with who you want to work with. It might come as a shock to you but you're usually your own ideal client.

Think back to when you first started out on your journey. What painful things happened to you? What turning points changed your life? Think about clients that you may have already worked with. What are their turning points? Think about the things that they say, "Wow, I never realized I did X, Y and Z, until I came to you." These are some of the pains that you're going to be digging into.

I want you to be like a dentist; get your hook out, and really knock on those painful teeth. Make them leap in pain! Find what it is that is so upsetting for them. What is the transformation that they want to have? For example, my clients' pains are that they're not making enough money and need more clients —plain and simple. What they really need is to make sales, but no one really wants to talk about sales. Behind their pain is their true desires, their pleasures. Most of my clients really want to be able to retire their husband. I'm not even quite sure why people want to do that. I love mine going to work each day, but many women want their hubbies to be at home with them. So, that's me getting out of my own head there. I don't want to retire my husband, but loads of my clients do. So, I need to talk about retiring husbands as a pleasurable place for them to get to.

They want to be able to take their families on holiday. They want to be able to pay and contribute back to their household. Many of them want to be famous. They do! They want to be seen as an authority in their industry. So, when you understand their pleasures, you can talk about moving them from the painful place they're in, to the pleasurable place. You want to take them from sitting on the couch, lonely, starving, wanting chocolate, and move them forward to being excited to be eating fine chocolate feeling loved!

GET MOMENTUM KEY POINTS

1. People are moved into action by the fear of pain and by the promise of pleasure.
2. What is it your clients really want? You can identify it by hitting on their pain points.
3. Once you understand their pain points and identify their true desires, you can move them into pleasure through your transformational process or product.

CHAPTER 11:

Know your real numbers. Cha-ching.

Now you have your ideal clients, you know what they want and what they need, you know what your skills are, and you've created your hot offer. It's now time to put that bad boy out into the marketplace and get some sales. "Woo hoo," says you *and* your bank account. It's about time.

First things first—it's really important in creating your $100k in 100 days to know what your numbers are.

Most females avoid numbers like the plague. They absolutely cannot stand it, and I say to my clients all the time, "It's very important that you get comfortable with your numbers." If there's some discomfort about understanding your sales figures—and what you're driving for and what your operational costs are and how much profit you're making—I want you to go back to the tips on money blocks in the Woo section of this book. Really dig into why you're feeling blocked around knowing your numbers for your business. Because at the end of the day, knowing your numbers and what you're striving for is going to one) bring in that vibrational energy, and two) makes you feel so powerful that you're in control.

A very close and dear friend of mine, Rebecca Button has a fantastic simplistic saying, "The more hands you shake, the more money you make." And that is 100% true.

Most people would like to think that they can manifest three or four people on to their list, turn them all in to clients and voilà they have a thriving business. This stems from the idea touted by big marketers saying, "The gold is in your list," which is true. However the real gold is the *connections* in your list. It's not just about collecting people's names and emails, and having a ginormous list of names that you think you're going to convert when you put an offer out. You need to have connected and *engaged* people in your list for them to want to buy from you. You need to shake their hands.

It would be easy for me to say to you that you will sell between one and five percent of your list. Say you have a thousand people on your list. That means you will statistically sell your product or service to ten of those people. Here's the but: if you have a thousand people on your list and none of them actually opens an email from you (because you're inconsistent in emailing them or you emails are going to the junk folder because they haven't whitelisted your email address) then those numbers of one to five percent are not going to ring true when you send out a sales email, right? Therefore, it's important that you're really, really honest with yourself when recording your numbers. Focus on engaged list numbers.

I'm going to tell you a little story to illustrate this exact conundrum. I'm terrible at comparing myself to other people. A self-professed numbers nerd, I love the external accolades that numbers bring. It's one of my love languages. With eighteen Ironmans, forty marathons, and three ultra-marathons behind me, I'm all about understanding the numbers—how much faster I can go, how much more I can get out of my gear, what my heart rate is. When it comes to business, I'm exactly the same.

Understandably, I was really put out that other people in the first group program I was part of had thousands of people on their list, yet I only had about two hundred. What was going on? Obviously, they had done some different attraction marketing type stuff that I wasn't privy to! I thought 'this is just rubbish'. I really beat myself up about it. 'Why was my list not growing as fast as everyone else's?' There was a huge amount of comparison. I became really angry, and then very depressed about it.

Fast forward to a few months later when I became involved in the promotion of an affiliate program. I found many of the big names that were also selling Gabrielle Bernstein's Sprit Junkie had thousands of people on their list and in their Facebook groups, but actually had a worse sales result than I did. All because they were just collecting names and numbers and not creating relationships with their people. There weren't creating any engagement. They weren't creating a connection with them. So, while I was comparing the top line number and thinking I was doing poorly, in fact I was winning. Why? Because I had a more engaged community. So, by knowing your engaged numbers, you can predict your level of sales and stay sane in your own head.

I want you to remember that whenever somebody gives you a statistic or any numbers that you need to hit to sell X-amount from, they need to be part of a connected community—active people. It's not just the size of your list.

As the saying says, "The more hands you shake, the more money you make". It's not 'the more people you put yourself in front of, the more money you make'. It's the more *hands you shake.*

How are you connecting with your audience to keep them active and excited so that when you do make an offer, they already like, love, and trust you enough to buy? What was really important in my $100k in 100 days was really engaging with my list and my Facebook Group. I did this by making sure that I was giving a lot of value.

I want you to lay out your numbers; you must know what you need to hit for each month. Start with the year. What would you like to achieve in a year? You should know this from some of your big dreams and goals in the Woo section. Say it's $100,000 in 100 days. How many units do you need to sell within that time to hit $100k?

You can hit $100k in many ways. For example –
10 x $10k
20 x $5k
50 x $2k
100 x $1000
200 x $500

Once you know how many units you need to sell, work backwards knowing that between one and five percent of your engaged list will buy. To get that five percent higher depends on how engaged your list is. Know how many people you must have on your list that are engaged and connected to hit your $100k goal.

To know how engaged your list is, you need to look at the open rates of your emails or stats in your social platforms. For example, if you have a list of a thousand people and your open rate is 8%, then only eighty people are looking at your email. If you sell to 1% of these eighty – that is 0.8 of a person! Therefore you want engagement to be as high as possible so you're getting your message (and product) in front of as many people as possible. Also note some of the engaged audience are going to be your mom and your sister and your cousins and your aunty, so don't count those!

By knowing your numbers, you can see how you can be realistic in setting your financial goals and have a better understanding of how much you need to grow to hit your goals. To hit the bigger goals you'll need to push yourself and get yourself out there more.

All this number talk might be quite the frightening exercise for you. You might put this book down and say, 'ugh, I really do not want to look at numbers, it just confuses me' and never pick the book up again. I implore you not to do that, because you won't grow in your business. You won't hit $100K in 100 days as easily as you would if you had a goal and knew the path to it. If you need a kick up the butt and you need a bit of a motivating, helping hand, get on over to www.pennyelliott.com/contact and I will give you a boot kicking session where we will help you work out what your numbers are and how you can realistically move forward to hit your targets.

It's important to remember money is the life blood of any business. To make it less daunting just think of money as a number. You must keep track of the money number. I don't mean you should be tight with it; you must invest to grow. However it must be said there needs to be a midway points between frivolous and flaunting it.

By knowing your numbers you can confidently say, "I can spend X amount of dollars to attract a client for X amount sale." For example, I spent $8,000 on Facebook ads to achieve $100K in 100 days. Yes, I spent $8k, but I got $100,000 back! That return on investment was totally profitable and one I do all day long. I knew what I was spending, how engaged my growing list was and therefore had some level of predictable certainty in the sales amount coming in.

Whereas, if I said to you that you need to spend $8,000 on Facebook ads in the next 100 days and not track it, but just watch it go out, you'd probably be mortified at the thought of spending your cash without knowing that you are going to get the money back. So, tracking your investment and knowing how that turns into more money through sales to your growing community is key. It's also a very rad process to watch - money truly grows like trees.

So you've kept reading on – well done, proud of you. Unfortunately knowing your numbers is not just a once-a-year exercise just for the tax man. Make the process fun! I want you to review your numbers every week on a Friday before you pour yourself that glass of wine. It will either be a celebratory wine or it might be a creative wine, or sometimes even a cry-in-your-wine party.

The celebratory wine is the 'yes, I'm crushing it wine'.

The creative wine is when you look at your numbers and they are not quite where you need them to be, so you think, "Right, what can I do to really make myself more visible and more out there, more hands shaken?".

And the cry-in-your-wine party is for when it's been a shit week and you need to take a chill pill and just relax, Go back to the Woo Section and find your centre again.

Jump over to the free workbook at
www.pennyelliott.com/book to use the quick spreadsheet that

I use every week to keep track of my numbers. This tracker makes it easy to see the growth or the pitfalls. I use it to help direct my team to what we need to work on the following week to get the numbers going in the upward trajectory.

Note: you will not see your numbers grow every week. This is an unrealistic expectation and one that—if you stick to wanting to see—will put you in a trap, because you will feel dejected if they don't keep going up each week.

It's not always an upward trajectory. That's the nature of sales. Some weeks will be shit and you just need to have some creative wine instead of a celebration wine, and get yourself on track the following week. Therefore, doing it weekly—not monthly—will mean that you can catch yourself before it spirals completely out of control and get back on track to have a strong month.

GET MOMENTUM KEY POINTS

1. The more hands you shake, the more money you make. It's not about the numbers at the top of the funnel, but the ones with whom you engage.
2. Knowing your numbers ensures you know how many 'hands to shake' to achieve your goals.
3. Make time for Friday-wine-yay! Review your numbers over a glass of wine to celebrate or commiserate.

CHAPTER 12:

One Clear Offer.

When it comes to selling something, people often want to please everyone. They have many offers, so that they can actually get clients. I see it all the time. 'I've got this, and I've got that, and I've got this product, and I've got that service, and if you want to cut it this way, you can have it that way… And if you want to have two sessions, you can have this.' The list goes on and on and on. You only need to search through some people's websites and you can find maybe fifteen to twenty different offers. I'm going to tell you here – this is madness.

When I used to work at Lindt Chocolate, we had many, many offers, right? There is a chocolate bunny, there's a chocolate frog for Easter, there's a chocolate egg. Then there's dark chocolate, white chocolate, hazelnut chocolate. Then they all come in all sorts of different sizes. There's the 250-gram, 100-gram, 10-gram, and the 5-gram. You name it. They had it to suit all of the market.

When it came down to selling things online, I obviously came from this Fast-Moving Consumer Goods (FMCG) background and thought that I needed to make lots of offers to people as well, to suit all of the market.

So, when I first started my business,
I had business hours.
I had a group program,
I had a group mastermind,
I had a small group program,
I had one-to-one,
I then had a short one-to-one.

On the strategy sessions, I would offer people all of these different items. I thought this is great! I'd surely to get lots of clients because I had a solution for everyone. I had something that everyone wants. So, even if they say, "I can't afford the one on one package", I could easily offer business hours on an hourly rate and just offer them one hour and help them that way. I wanted to have an offer to suit everyone's needs, just like we did at Lindt.

Yet, having all these offers was just causing confusion. A confused mind says no.

Here's the reason - the person on the other end of the phone or Zoom call is looking to you as the consultant, the leader; they are looking to you to be the informant, and to lead them to the right decision. Yet, with a thousand offers, you're giving them the power to decide. But they don't know what they need— that's why they contacted you in the first place!

Yet, so many women don't want to have one offer or feel like they're pushing people into a solution that doesn't exactly suit all of the clients wants. A lot of women that come to me feel having one offer is quite deceptive and so, would rather leave the decision to the buyer.

Here's where I want to reframe that for you. There's a difference between pushing someone into a solution that won't work for them just so you can make a sale verses actually leading them into the right decision that supports their journey. At the end of the day, you want the decision to be hers completely. But, when people are trying to make a big shift in their life—whether it's through weight loss, mindset changes, relationships, business, finances, or whatever it is— they are coming to you because you're a lot further ahead than them and can help them achieve accelerated results.

They trust your knowledgeable position and what you suggest to be their next steps. To do this, you need to listen to them, understand what they have, and what they need, and then make them one solid offer to solve their issue.

Let me illustrate this to you on another way: Oprah Winfrey is an amazing American woman with huge natural talent discovered in the movie Purple Rain. She has gone on to be one of the most influential women in the world alongside Mother Teresa. She has her own television show, her own film production, magazine, underpants, candles, tea, magazine and even a cruise ship and travel agency all under her Oprah Winfrey branding.

When she first started out though, she was an actor, and then had her TV show and she stood for one thing, one thing only and that was her TV show. From that, she started to branch out and do all the other passion projects that she desired. Because she was known for this one thing—being an influential black woman with her own television show and asking the hard-hitting controversial questions helping to uplift the spirits of all people in general, she is now able to sell anything she likes. When she wanted to sell underpants, everyone thought, "Wow, Oprah Winfrey, I know her. She's amazing. I already trust her; these underpants must be amazing if she says they are!".

Here's a famous quote that Oprah has in her book *What I Know for Sure*, "Stick with what you know best, until you don't need to do it anymore. Then try something new." That's it. This is why you want to be known for your one offer. This is often hard as our creativity is the reason we become entrepreneurs. Because we have all these amazing ideas; we see a problem and we know how to fix it a bazillion different ways.

However, on the other hand, if you want to flip the coin over, being too creative and having too many ideas can also be the demise of many entrepreneurs.

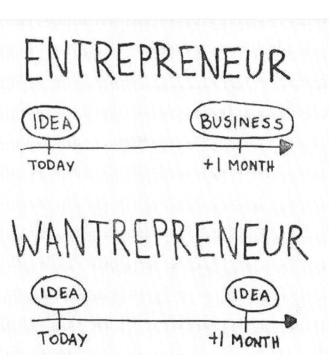

Having too many ideas only leads to confusion both to you and the people you're trying to attract. What you want to do is have one solid offer and be known for that one thing.

I want you to think of your business like a tree. A tree can't grow fruit, or flowers, or leaves until its seed is planted deep into the soil and is growing a really strong trunk. From that strong trunk grows the leaves and the branches, and then from that grows the fruit of the flowers. I want you to see your business exactly like this metaphor. You need to plant that seed—that one idea in your business, that one signature thing that you're known for. First, it grows a tall, strong trunk. As

123

you know with growing trees, this may take a few years, not seconds. From that strong trunk comes branches. Similarly, once you have your strong one offer you can then branch out in different branches and have different fruits, because you are known so well that people will trust you and will try these other things you produce.

So, I want you to look at your business and ask yourself:

- How many offers do I have?
- Am I confusing my audience?
- Can I tie this down to one main offer?
- Am I being too wishy-washy?

To take it one step further—within that one offer, I want you to have three different levels of support. Don't worry; it will all makes sense soon—we're getting into why you need three different levels of support soon. Just know you need these levels.

For example, if you want to join the *Get Momentum Mastermind* there's 15 masterclasses and a hundred days of support through a closed group. If you want extra support on top of that, you can join the VIP, which gives you a fortnightly half-an-hour call with myself or one of my coaches where you can receive bespoke one-to-one support. Then, if you want to go next level, you go into full one-to-one support where you have four months of complete access to me via email and phone calls. Here you have three levels of support within one offer.

So, within your signature program—offer, product, whatever it is—I want you to have three different levels. We're gonna come to why you must have three different levels in a future chapter, but for now, just pick your one thing to get those three different mini-levels within there.

GET MOMENTUM KEY POINTS

1. The riches are in the niches!
2. Start by creating authority in your niche by having one offer before you try to sell everything to everyone.
3. Create three sub-levels of support within your offer.

CHAPTER 13:

Vibe and Tone

When it comes to selling things, it's really important to have the right vibe and the right tone. As we discussed earlier, people are buying your confidence. People are buying your leadership. They want to know that you are the shit when it comes to what you're selling.

Now, so many times—and this is one of the prime reasons why I have started helping women with the growth of their businesses and sales coaching—is because I kept hearing what I call "the little girl voice".

You might be on a great phone conversation, or having a great conversation in a store with someone, and they're like, "Oh yeah, this is really amazing. It's gonna change your life, and this is how it works, and this is how I've used it in the past, and duh, duh, duh, dah," and be really excited about it. When it comes to the price bit, females are drastically different to men. Men will just say, "This is what the price is. It's $10,000," and be quiet to let the other party take in the investment level and reply. I know this from working with many men in the technical industry in my previous sales and marketing roles.

What was astonishingly different when I started working with females, I noticed that they would hang their head and bring out what I call "the little girl voice" when it came to talking about the price. "Well, you know, it's like, um, well it's like $1,000, but you know what? I know that you're going through a tough time at the moment, so I'll give you 50% off and you can pat my cat for free, oh and don't worry about paying me right now, it's ok – just get it to me when you can. I can also throw in my car for free." They just give it all away and more. They lose the tone, they lose the vibe of the conversation, they lose their confidence and they absolutely undersell themselves.

The person on the other end of the phone or the other end of the conversation is all excited about this product or service, and then when it comes to the money part, they're like, "That's a bit weird. Why are they so under-confident around the price? Is there something that they're hiding?"

This is when you get that, "Oh, I'll think about it," or, "I need to go and talk to my husband, my brother, my mother, my pet guinea pig," you'll hear all the excuses under the sun. You hang up, and you think, "That's strange. They seemed really keen and then suddenly they weren't," you think it's them, but actually it's yourself. It's your own vibe and tone.

I've got an example of this; say you're going to buy a two-litre bottle of milk. You go into the store, and you say, "Oh, they've got this new A2 milk available." Say it's "A2," the new fancy milk that's out. "Oh, I might give that a try." So, you walk to the checkout, and it's not a self-service, there's actually someone there who's going to talk to you. They say, "Oh, that's the new milk." You're like, "Yeah, I thought I'd give it a try." And they're like, "Oh yeah, well, I don't know. It looks a bit funny don't you think?" Then you're like, "Oh no, I thought it looked alright." And they're like, "Mm, yeah. Wow, and it's $9 for the two litres." "Oh, okay."

You pay for it because you're in the queue, right and can't just dump it and leave? You go home, and you make your cup of tea, and put the milk in it, and you're like, "Mm, not really sure if it tastes that good or not." Maybe you have cereal the next day, and when you pour some milk in, you think, "I don't think it's even that much better than the other stuff. I'm not really sure it's worth the $9." You never buy the A2 milk again. You go back to the brand that you used to buy and never think about A2 again.

Scenario two. You go into the store, you see this A2 milk. Exactly the same milk, same container, same packaging, everything, and you grab a two-litre bottle and go to the checkout. You go to pay, and you get a different salesperson, and they say, "Wow, that's that new A2 milk. I heard it's really awesome. It's so good. It's much easier on your gut, and it tastes really yummy. Oh, that stuff looks amazing. Oh, and it's only $9—bargain! It's so cheap for your health. Oh, my goodness. I can't believe it. It's so good. Loads of people have been buying it. It's absolutely fantastic. You'll really enjoy that." You leave the store with a little bit of a skip, and you think, "Can't wait to go home and try it." You make a cup of tea, and you instantly feel a whole heap better because you've been using this A2 milk. You're totally sold on A2 milk and buy it forever more, no matter the price. This is your new milk and you're making your life just that bit healthier each day with your choice.

Now, the milk's exactly the same. The container's exactly the same. The packaging is *exactly* the same. The price is *exactly* the same. The only thing that is different in those two scenarios is the vibe and the tone of the salesperson. One instilled doubt in you and the other one instilled confidence in you that this was the right decision and purchase to make.

So, when it comes to making sales in your business—and on your journey to $100k in 100 days—I want you to really think about your vibe and tone. I want you to be really sure of yourself and what you're selling.

Now, this is not a natural skill set, and most people don't get into business to become really good at sales. But unfortunately, if you don't have any sales in your business, then you don't have a business. You might think that's a really harsh thing to say, but it is true. You just have a pretty website and fun on Instagram. That's all. What you need is sales coming in.

You do need to be really good at sales. No-one sells you, or your business, or your services like you do. So, you must master your sales first before you can outsource it. A lot of people become quite upset by that fact, but it's true. You need to master sales yourself before you can train anyone else to master it.

However to get good is really easy. All you need to do is practise. If you are trying to sell your services and you don't know your prices or your offer then how will you train someone else to sell them for you? From the previous chapters you will know your numbers and you will know your offer. Now all that is left to do is to sit in front of the mirror and practice, practice, practice.

Just like when you were a kid and you learned how to brush your teeth. You didn't know how to brush your teeth when you first started, but you practised it morning and night, morning and night, morning and night, until it is now second nature for you for the whole of your life.

You can now brush your teeth with your eyes closed. SIDE NOTE - I dare you. Tonight, when you go to brush your teeth, try and brush them with your eyes closed, and I'm sure that you will do a perfectly good job as you would do staring at yourself in the mirror. It's because you've practiced it again, and again, and again.

I want you to feel like this about selling your products or services, just like brushing your teeth. You should feel as though you can do it with your eyes closed. You know your numbers; you know exactly what you're gonna say, and you can say it with the same high energy and excitement that you do when you're talking about how you can help people, and how you can be in service to them. There's no drop off when you say the price. I want you to be able to confidently tell people, "It's $10,000 to work with me one-on-one, and the reason for that is because you get me in your back pocket. You get me in the corner of your boxing ring. I'll be 100% all there for you," and not have any drop in tone or worse still totally freak out and not even say the price!

The only way that you're gonna understand, or be able to reflect on this, is if you record yourself. I want you to record yourself as you are in a sales conversation, play it back and listen to the tone more than the words. If you want to do this with someone else, jump into the Get Momentum Entrepreneurs Facebook group, here you will be able to ask for a buddy to be able to do some practice sales calls with. You guys can take turns - one person be the sales person, and one person be the customer, and then swap over. Record the session and then you'll be able to see how your voice drops, or how you dilly-dally around the pricing, or the money investment piece.

If there is any dilly-dallying, or little girl voice, I want you to go back to the Woo section of this book, and really work on any money blocks coming up. Are there any feelings of doubt that you're not worth it, who's going pay that to work with me, any of those self-doubting prophecies that are there. Changing those will help increase your vibe and your tone.

People need to feel confident to buy from you. That confidence comes from you only. Get your confident pants on, girl!

GET MOMENTUM KEY POINTS

1. Know your worth! If you don't, you won't be able to instil confidence in your potential clients.
2. Mind the little-girl voice or drop in tone when you talk about the price of your offer.
3. Join the Get Momentum Entrepreneurs Facebook group for support to practise your sales conversations with ladies that care.

CHAPTER 14:

Sales Structure

This is one of the most important sections of this book. You will want to put a bookmark in here, get out your highlighters and absorb this chapter. Reread it, reuse it, and by the time that you have really succeeded in the $100K in 100 days these pages should definitely be well-worn.

I want to introduce you to the Container Sales method. But before I tell you what the method is, I want you to hear from a couple of people who found this an absolute life-changing, game-changer sales technique for their business.

Meet Sarah. She is one kick-ass entrepreneur. She is the e-commerce Queen, ex-Raw Food Mumma straight out of Australia who helps people take their e-commerce business from six to seven figures. Before trying the container sales method, she really thought that people in e-commerce didn't have the money to be able to spend on high level coaching. Now, while a lot of this thought pattern is in the Woo section (think - money block), it can also be the way that you are making your offer to your prospective customer.

And in this case, it was exactly both! Firstly, she needed to believe in herself, her services, and her ability. She's the best in Australia if not Down Under at e-commerce coaching, a quick look at the results she got for her clients and she started to believe this fact. Secondly, it's all about how she was delivering her sales message. By using this Container Sales method, she went from not quite sure if she was charging too much—and whether people could afford her—to signing fifteen people in one month in to her high end mastermind. Using this method she has really rocketed forward with confidence that she has the skills to offer people what they want in such a way that it isn't really pushy.

The Container Sale method is the easiest format for you to use with absolutely any sales conversation. You do however need several levels of support for the person; so think about the different products, services, or programs you offer, and how they tier from the largest investment—which is usually the most amount of support—right down to the least amount of support and the least amount of investment.

Why we call this a Container Sale is because instead of just saying, "Would you like this product, or this service, or this program?", it's about, "Which level of support would you like?" You very rarely get a 'no' in this situation. It's a very simple step. This type of questioning opens up a conversation instead of a straight offer where they can only say yes or no.

First, I want you to do a bit of research on the person so that you know who you're speaking to, especially if they haven't filled out an application form. If they filled out an application form, then you're going to have some great information already. If they haven't, then it's good to have a bit of a stalk around, and we're very lucky and fortunate in the internet world to be able to do that so that you can connect with them when you're on the call.

Make sure that you're in a quiet environment, and that you are mentally ready for the call. You don't think, "Grr, I've got to get this call done so that I can get on with something else more important." Really see sales as service, and be in service to that person by being relaxed and ready.

Also, know that *they're* probably very apprehensive about talking to you for two reasons. One, they're probably going to think that you're a bit of a superstar in the area that they want to improve in; they're going to be a bit intimidated by you, and two they're probably going to also be apprehensive about the changes that are coming down the pipeline. Even though they're going to be positive changes, people always are apprehensive.

Think about the little kid who goes and talks to their teacher, right? They're always very, very shy the first time and not quite sure what they can ask their teacher. It's the same situation, so make sure you're very, very welcoming when people get on the call with you. Make sure you're radiating a high-vibration, and keep it there. They will raise up to you.

The first thing I want you to do is to really connect with them, and I want you to really spend a bit of time here in this—I call it the chit-chat. But really, the longer you spend here, the more comfortable they feel to go deeper with you in the call about their pain points and what they want to achieve.

A really simple way of doing this is to connect about things you have in common. We recognize we want our mentors and coaches to have done similar things to us further down the path. We want to work with people who have already gone and done what we desire to do, so it's really important that you empathise with where they are right now or have some way of connecting. If you think about it, wherever you travel around the world, you always meet someone from your local town, city, or country. You're like, "Hi," and you instantly are attracted to talk to them, because you are of a likeness.

That is human psychology. We all want to be liked by someone else, and usually, if we have similar interests, it's really easy to talk with people. This is easy to do from your snooping—say they have a dog and you also have a dog—you can say, "Well, actually, I saw on your profile picture you've got a dog. What sort of dog? I've got a dog, too. Isn't that great?" Then go into the call... Or you might say, "Oh, I see that you have children," or, "From your application form, you said you like working with blah, blah, blah people. Well, so do I! I think that is great," or whatever it might be. But really join the dots for them so that they feel comfortable connecting with you.

The second step is to find out what's not working for them. Obviously, at the beginning of the call, you want to see the pretence around how the call will roll, "Look, we're going to dive into where you are right now, what's not working, what is working. Then, if the fit is right, we're going to talk about how we can work together. Okay? Does that sound fine?" You get that little 'yes'. Remember, you're always looking for these mini yes's the whole way through the call.

So, then you find out what's not working for them. What are their struggles? Why are they struggles for them now? You're listening for the urgency. How urgently do they want these changes? At first, it's like, "Oh, that would be nice." That is not the real struggle. That is not the real urgency, and you can't really help someone with "Oh, it would be nice." If it's hot and painful right now, that is how you can help someone.

Then, you really want to spend a lot of time listening in this step, as it's actually the first step to overcoming objections. If you're not listening and asking lots of questions in this— "But why? But why? But why?" Like as a child, "But why? But why? But why?" then you're talking too much. Keep diving in deeper and listening. Obviously, don't say, "But why?" continuously like a child, move the question style. You can say, "So, tell me more. What is underneath that? What does that really mean to you? Why do you think you are where you are right now?"

Make sure that you keep asking these deeper questions so that you can start to hear phrases like, "I'm stuck. I've struggled. I don't have clarity. I'm bothered by," and the emotions that come with this phrases. This will be in their tone and vibe, which can only be heard.

Now, I cannot stress enough the importance of writing notes while on a call. Typing is sometimes off-putting. When you can hear someone typing, you think, "Oh, what are they typing, are they even listening to me?" If you're writing it down, it's much quieter. It's also a very good way for you and your brain to process things as well as you see it coming out on the paper. Look for the key emotions along the way and really understand what it is they're struggling with; why they have decided to explore making a change in their life.

Listen for the problem, and make sure you have something that can solve it. Do not jump into solving that problem right there and then on the phone. Listen, listen, listen, listen, listen. These days, people struggle to be heard. They struggle to find someone to listen to them. If you can actually sit and listen to someone for fifteen minutes—which is around how long this will take if the whole call is thirty-minutes long—they will just absolutely love that space to be heard right from the word 'go'. Because to be listened to is something that people—especially of this world, and this generation, and this time—are craving. You're going to gain a lot of respect just by listening and asking prompting questions.

Do not get into problem-solving. It is so easy to go, "Oh, I know the answer to that," and solve the problem. Do not problem-solve, okay? I cannot stress that enough. Just listen and keep asking those prompting questions. Keep getting them to dive deeper into themselves. You will see why – keep reading.

The next step is future-pacing. Think about where they want to go. So, you've really dug into the pain. Now, you want to see where they want to go, the results they crave. This is really important, because I've had one girl say that she really wanted to buy a pink castle and unicorns, and dress like a princess every day. That was her vision. And despite having no following, list or income she was adamite that this was her vision. No matter how hard I worked with her to get momentum in her business I could never give her the outcome she wanted.

I didn't offer to work with her because that would be setting both of us up to fail, right? Make sure that you get into the vision with them and really listen. Again, this is so important. Listen, listen, listen.

Most people have a desire for change to get to a place and that place is where you can help them with. In this step you're trying to help them understand what they truly desire. Now, behind that pink castle, and all the unicorns, and princesses, was probably actually a deep desire for her family to love her or for someone to notice and give her love, right? Make sure that you ask about their vision and the why behind the why. Remember, people buy people—not products, services, and programs—so it is ok to go deep with them on a call, be a human and help them verbalise where they want to be in 3, 6, 9 months from now.

The easiest way is to ask them, "Where would you like to be in X time?" and insert the time frame that your offer is. For my courses that would be 60 days for 60 Days to $3k, 100 Days for my Get Momentum Mastermind and 4 months for my one on one coaching.

I usually use the seasons as a timeline guide, for example – "where would you like to be by the end of summer," or "where would you like to be by the beginning of winter". You really need to get them to paint that vision and go in to details. Don't let them say '$10k months' or 'loose 5kg', really dig in to why they want $10k months, what would that do for them financially, psychologically, emotionally?

Now again, no solving their problems at this stage. Bite your tongue and don't let it happen. Put a big post-it note on your wall if you have to, but whatever you do don't jump in to problem solving mode!

The next step you do get to talk though! This step is all about showing you've been listening. Recap exactly where they're at right now and then where they want to go. Make sure you reflect back to them what they said. The easiest way to do this is by using their words, not yours, this is where your notes come in handy. People really hear what they said when it is in their words as it feels familiar to them. Then reflect back where they said they wanted to go and really amp up their vision to show them what is possible.

You really put colour on it, because most people overestimate what they can do in a year but underestimate what they can do in ten years: a Tony Robbins quote that I love. You really want to bring their desire to life, and you can be quiet theatrical about it, have fun!

For example, when I've spoken to other clients, a common theme is they want to create consistent $10K months so that they can reinvest back in their business and get momentum. That's quite a black and white vision with quantifiable outcomes. However, you can add some colour into it by saying, "So, what I'm hearing you say is you want to make consistent $10K months so that you can reinvest it back into your business. In doing so, you can hire someone else to complete the website that you've been trying to finish. You can get a design person to handle all your creative work, as you said this wasn't a strength of yours. $10k months would also give you the ability to have some VA support, freeing you from admin tasks so that you can spend time with your kids, knowing that everything is taken care of in your business. Having all this in place will give you that lifestyle of ease you crave. How awesome would that be?" See how I've reflected it back to them, but I've completely amped her desire for consistent $10k months?

Once you understand their vision, then you can, one, decide whether you want to work with them or not. It's up to you, not up to them, right? If it's not a good fit, then refer them on to someone else, "I don't think we're a good fit. I can't take you where you want to go, but I've got someone who can. Let me introduce you." Or just say, "Now I've heard where you're at I'm not a good fit. I can't take you where you want to go."

Side note here – DO NOT create an offer on the fly to meet their desires. This is not sticking to your core offer and is not in service to the person on the other end of the conversation. I have done this in the early stages of my business, thinking it would help them, including extended payment plans. ALL of them have failed to show up fully for the coaching and defaulted on payments. They were not ready and not committed. So learn from my mistakes! OK, back to the text.

Otherwise, if you are a good fit, then you move onto the next step, which is the invitation. This is where you say, "Okay, so this is great. Would it be cool if I share how I help my clients? I don't know if this would be helpful, but do you want to hear how I work with Phoebe, who was in a similar place?" Then, use an example of a previous client that you've helped in a similar starting place as the person on the phone.

Here is my example, "So, I have a client, Phoebe. She is a Pilates instructor with a team of girls that go to people's homes for 1:1 Pilates sessions. She wanted to have some consistency in her income each month, break through the five-figure mark monthly and not work any more hours, as she felt super burnt out. Together, we managed to reduce her hours from eighty to fifty by putting systems in place, hiring the right help, and delegating more to her team, all while making an extra $3K a month, taking her over the 5-figure threshold. That could easily be you. You could easily be in that situation as well. Instead of working 80 hours, we can reduce it down to 50, and I can show you ways that you can increase your revenue as well without just putting your prices up. Da, da, da, da, da." Show them their vision in a client example.

Then, the last piece of the sales puzzle is obviously delivering your offer, and this is where we talk about the Container Sale. Firstly, I want you to create a bridge after providing the client testimonial from where they are now, to being in the vision that they want. Position yourself as the vehicle that can drive them over that bridge. Next, I want you to talk them through your offers and *then* your pricing.

The way to move into the container without getting a little girl voice going, is to simply say, "Okay, so I really like where you've come from and where you're going (use their specifics in their language). I really think that we would make a great fit. Would you like to know how I worked with Phoebe? Because that could be you, too, right?" You're asking permission to pitch. That way, you're getting a yes and another yes. Remember - you want the mini yes's along the way. You always want all the yeses!

If they say no, you could say, "Oh, okay. Can I ask why?" Don't be afraid to ask why and just hang up the phone. They're likely to say, "Well, actually, I don't want to do this anymore," or come up with an objection based in fear. Go back to the probing questions and listening.

Now, you get onto your Container. I want you to have three offers ready:

Offer #1: The highest value of investment and highest amount of support.
Offer #2: A medium investment and mid-range level of support.
Offer #3: The lowest support and lowest investment.

When you are saying your offers I want you to go in that order—high to low. For example, my pitch goes something like this: "Okay, so the crème de la crème way of working with me is to have the one-to-one mentorship. It's four months. We work together, and I take you from confused to a consistent income module. Together we actually set up systems so that you can Get Momentum, and your business doesn't run you."

Then, I'll say, "You'll get full email access to me. You'll have forty-five-minute calls three times a month." I often say three times a week, and have to say 'I always get that wrong! It's three times a month.' "You also get full access to any of my materials, courses and masterclasses." Depending on who the person is, I will give them a tech tutorial library if their tech is not great. Also, I've given templates to use with their VAs, whatever they have said they need and I have they'll get.

Then I say, "Okay, so that's the crème de la crème, right? The next one is to come into my mastermind, the *Get Momentum Mastermind*. We've got some amazing women in this community. It's a hundred days, and it's all about creating the same $100k in 100 days that I personally did. You get ten masterclasses from me, one a week. You get the support of the Private Facebook group, which has some amazing other business women in too. We have a live call each week where you can ask any questions you'd like. You also get all my templates, and all my worksheets to use within your own business. You'll also receive a plan to create a five figure funnel that coverts cold leads in to buyers."

And I continue, "Then, we also have masterclasses on the most profitable way to make sales online and another of the easiest automated way to make sales online. We also track your fitness and health because it's really important to get that balanced lifestyle as a business owner so that we don't get burnout, because it's not about the 80 to 100-hour weeks. Okay? That's the medium level of support. There's no email access to me, and there's no phone calls unless you want to go VIP."

And the last one; "Then, the last level of support is 60 days to $3K, which is a group program. There are Q&A times once a week where you can ask whatever you want. You get four modules, which includes growth and money mindset because it's really important to have that rock solid first. You also get training on how to find leads organically through authentic outreach and different types of techniques to be able to get clients without advertising. We then talk about setting up your first freebie offer and landing page, and we have video tutorials, and then driving some traffic to that through some Facebook ads."

I let them say "Hmmm" or "Okay", and then I continue, "You also get a bonus mini marketing makeover on your website so that your pages actually sell and isn't just holding a place in the atmosphere. You'll also get some sales call training as a bonus as well. That's for sixty days."

Then, I take a big, deep breath because they've just taken on heaps of information—like you just have reading this—and I then say, "How does it feel?"

Now they can only say, "All right. Okay. Well, that sounds really cool. I like the sound of …," and then you can then just guide them to that exact level of support they like. They can't say no, as it's not a yes no question. It's about how they feel.

So, did you notice that I didn't use any of the prices in those descriptions? We want people to base themselves on what level of support they like, and then if they say, "Well, I like the one-to-one, but what's the investment level?" They don't want you to go back through exactly what you just said in this container of three offers, but you say what the investment is. Right? "So, would it be helpful if we talk about the dollars and cents?"

Then, people will always say, "Yes, of course. I need to know the price," This is the green light you want. Re-describe the offers in detail again and include the price at the end. It may sound like you're repeating yourself (you are!) but it's important so they don't just hear the price, but hear the value attached. I also make sure I reassure what they said they didn't want and how the program will fix their pain, "And just remember the program is great for people who don't want to struggle with X, Y, and Z. In fact, I love it because I get to help you with A, B, C." When you announce your investment level again, start at the highest price point for the largest amount of support, then the middle, then the lowest with the low support. Does that all make sense?

You want to start at the highest and move down to the lowest because otherwise, people perceive it to be increasingly expensive, right? It's much easier to start at the top and go down, but do not say, "My one-to-one is $10,000. The Get Momentum Mastermind is $3,997, and the 60 days to $3K is $1,497. Right?"

It is KEY to not say just the prices alone because all people hear is the price, and they don't hear the value and the support that's associated to it. You need to go back through, and you're going to sound like a parrot going back through all this stuff, but people need to hear things more than once, especially if they're making a big investment and a big change in their world. They need to re-hear exactly what it is that's within that container of offers to feel confident to make a decision.

After some practise from you, suddenly, they'll start to say "Okay. I understand why the one-to-one is $10,000, because you get absolutely everything, right? That totally makes sense now, and why $3K to 60 days if $1,497." It removes the ability for people to flatly say, "No, I don't want to work with you," or, "I can't afford it.". They now have three different levels to choose from.

It is here that you can bring up payment plans if you have any. Do not talk about them any earlier though as it is super confusing to the person who is already taking in a lot of information.

Then, you can go through some of the trial closes until you get their credit card details and payment. You can also break it down for them to see how the investment will pay off – for example, "If you make $10,000 in four months, and then you make another $10,000 in the next four months, you've doubled your investment, right? This coaching has paid for itself and the skills you've learnt stay with you to keep making money and momentum.

Another example is a dietician. Her Container might be to have her send texts every day on meal plans and come virtually grocery shopping with you on FaceTime each week. Her next level of support could be a group program for sisterhood support and generic meal plans. Her lowest level of support might be a downloadable 8 week course of meal plans to do yourself. Her trial close could be the cost of a stomach band versus the cost of her personalised program.

Never guarantee results, though. This is a big trap for woman! Never make a guarantee like, "Okay. Well, if you pay the first $2,997 payment and then work really hard for the month doing everything I say, you'll be able to make the money for the next month's payment." Take my advice on this! That will never play to your advantage. It's a very, very dangerous game to play because then, the reliance comes back onto you to get them results. Yet remember, the reliance is on them to do the work. It's a fifty-fifty relationship, and you both have to work on achieving the goals.

Think about the gym. Imagine you go and see a PT, and you tell him, "Oh, I want to lose 5 kilograms."

PT says, "Cool, do this program. You should lose 5 kgs easily in a month."

But hang on. You go to the gym, and you work really hard, and then you go home. You eat a packet of Tim Tams. The next day, you eat a pizza, and the day after that, you go out on a bender and have six glasses of wine and two cocktails. Then, you think, "Shit, I'm going to see my PT in two days' time," and so you eat clean for two days. When you weigh yourself and you haven't lost any weight. Is it that your PT's program isn't working? It's not the PT's fault, right? It's your fault because you haven't eaten clean the whole way through.

It's exactly the same with your programs, your products, or your services. You're not sitting with the person making them do every single thing that you say, suggest, or that the course offers, or that the product says it will do, right? There's never a guarantee. You can however give them a trial period. You can give them some money back if they are really unhappy and they've proven they have done all that you have given to them.

In the 60 days to $3K, we've never ever had anyone ever remotely worry about the 14 day money back guarantee. We have girls hitting the $3K mark all the time, a 98% success rate. They get on the Awards page, and they receive a special award in the post from me. I've also said that if they get to $5K within the sixty days, they get $1,000 credit towards working one-to-one with me.

You too can get creative with incentives to show how sure you are about your product, or your service, or your package, but never, ever guarantee definitive results.

Back to the Container Sales. Once they've decided which level of support they want, they might say, "Oh, I'd really love to be in a Get Momentum Mastermind, but I'm not at $5K months," or, "I'd really love to do the one-to-one mentorship, but I feel that I'm more at the level of $3K to 60 days," which is totally cool. Once they get to that $5K, they get that $1,000 credit to work with me one-on-one, so that makes sense, right? That helps people move up through the value ladder.

That's why this Container Sales system is a really, really lovely approach. It gives people the opportunity to choose what feels fab for them. It's an authentic conversation about support.

When they say, "Yup, that's great," you move on to the final step. In our case, as we take payment on the phone, we then send them a contract if it's one-to-one. If it's one of the Get Momentum Mastermind or 60 Days to $3k programs, then they check a box to agree to the terms and conditions. We then give them instant access into the Facebook group, instant access into the membership area, and send them over the welcome pack. It's really important to give them their product straight away. Is stops what is called buyer's remorse. Send it while you're on the phone with them. Make sure they don't just hang up the phone, and then be like, "Shit, what the hell have I just done?" and go into a complete frazzled downward spiral.

I've had that happen with one lady. She joined a group program a long, long time ago. She paid the smallest amount of the payment plan options that we had. Then I was bombarded with a doubtful, fearful messages into my Messenger because we hadn't let her into the Facebook group instantly. "My god, what have I done? This is dreadful. I don't think I'm good enough. I don't think I'm even going to make it."

We hadn't welcomed her properly. We hadn't given her anything straight away, and she just went into a complete spiral of fear and negative self-talk. I felt so bad! It was dreadful because I didn't support her enough by explaining what the next steps were, what she could expect and then following through with those promptly! It was completely my fault, and she ended up wanting to be taken out of the course.

Obviously, I offered her a refund straight away, and I don't even think she wanted it, because she felt so bad that she had made this really terrible decision. In reality, she made a fantastic decision to step forward and go for her dreams. I'm sure she's probably still in exactly the same place she was in now, three years later.

Remember when you're taking people through these calls, they go really deep. If you're digging up their internal desires, they probably haven't even expressed those to themselves before, so it's really important that you support them right through not only the call but the delivery. If you're sending them a product, make sure you send them a product description in an email—or you give them an estimated time, and the support number if they haven't got it, or a tracking number on the package.

Alrighty, so that is Container Sales, and that is one of the sweetest ways to be in service to someone and help them make a decision to work with you.

GET MOMENTUM KEY POINTS

1. Stalk your leads (nicely, of course) and find a way to connect with them on a personal level during the first few minutes of the call. This will save you hours in the long run.

2. Create three offers with varying support and investment levels, and pitch them from highest investment and support to the lowest. Be sure to mention your instalment options at the end to avoid confusion, but never make any guarantees on results.

3. Offer them reassurances as soon as they have paid, whether it's a welcome email, a tracking number, or an introduction video to avoid buyer's remorse.

CHAPTER 15:

Taking You Online in Automation

The Nirvana of making sales while you sleep—or while you rest, or while you're playing with your family—is the huge draw card that makes women flock to online sales. It is the freedom profit model that everyone is after; freedom to be able to do whatever you want, when you want to, and to still have money coming in.

Now, to achieve this Nirvana you need to be selling online. You now know how to create a Container Sale and feel uber confident it's now time to automate the lead generation machine in your business.

I'm going to tell you a little story about how I had a client come to me who was really, really tired of networking. There were only so many hours in a day that this lady could actually get out while having a family and a husband and all the other commitments that go with life. She wanted to be able to leverage her current networks, but also wanted to know how she could go further with her business. Basically she'd put a ceiling on herself, because there was only so far that she could travel to meet new people. She had tapped out her local area yet she wanted to be able to make $100k in 100 days. She also couldn't fathom how to charge more to the people that in her immediate network.

So, we spoke about actually broadening her network instead of raising her prices. Initially, this was a real mind shift for her yet within the 100 days that we worked together in the *Get Momentum Mastermind*, she began to find clients that she'd never heard of before from all over the world. She was full of glee at these new faces and how easy it was. So, how did she do this? She took her business online.

Now, it is a really bold statement of me to simply say 'take your business online', because sometimes when you take your business online, it can actually end up causing you more headaches than not with the huge increase in sales and the accompanying admin that goes with the growth.

But if you spend the time automating processes you will cope with this influx with grace. One key thing that I really focused on in the $100K in 100 days was to get automation happening in every area of my business. As you know, I'm located in beautiful New Zealand, which is down in the bottom of the world. Although so far away, we're actually twelve hours ahead of Greenwich Mean Time (GMT), which means that yes, I do see the sunrise before everyone else in the world; but it also means that while most of the world is awake, we're sound asleep. (or not as the case maybe finishing this chapter!) So that means that the amount of time that I can be physically visible to people around the globe is restricted. It really just is the few hours in the morning that I wake up.

So, to be able to have $100k in 100 days or insert your big dream goal here, you need to have a simple funnel with nurturing emails. I'm going to walk you through the exact diagram seen here:

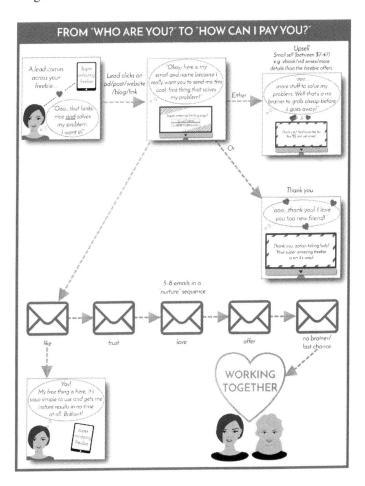

First, you need to have a landing page. Now, to be clear a landing page isn't your website. The best platform to use is ClickFunnels. Trust me, I have used all of them. I've tried Leadpages, Unbounce, Mail Chimp, SquareSpace. I've also tried HubSpot. But none do all the functions that ClickFunnels offers. The main reason I am affiliated with and use ClickFunnels, is it is easy to use and gives you all the statistics that you need to trouble shoot and scale. The support is ginormous, it's unbelievable and there's a lot of funnels in the software that are already built for you. All you have to do is tweak and change them to have your messaging in there.

If you use the link down below to set up your fourteen-day free trial, we'll see that you come up on our list and I will give you the exact funnel that we are talking about right now. How rad is that?!

www.pennyelliott.com/click-funnels-affiliate

You'll actually be able to read this chapter and step your way through the exact funnel 'I'm writing about right now. Cool, huh?! And it's free, cause that's how I roll—with high vibe and tone... ;)

So, why is it important to have a landing page instead of a website? I get this question so many times. The difference is that when you're sending people to a landing page the only objective is to get their name and email address. When you send people to your website, they have all the different tabs to scroll through and often get lost in in your website sight.

Now, think about your own behaviours here. How many times do you go to a website and click around, and think, "Oh, this is great, and that's great..." Then, you click out of the website and all of a sudden you're down a rabbit hole somewhere else? You can't actually remember what you were looking at to start with!

When it comes to sales online, you want people to come to this landing page and only be offered that one thing. You just want to have the next step: click the button and say "Yes, I would like to purchase/opt in/book a call."

When you are sending people to the top of a sales funnel, you are generally giving something away for free to start with. You want to give away loads of value first. It's like a dating; you don't want to jump straight into bed with someone on the first date. You want to ask them out for coffee, give them movie tickets, and keep moving forward building on the last step of trust. Until you actually ask them to come home with you, which is the purchase.

There will be some people, however, that will want to jump straight into bed with you, right away. Let's be honest, we all know we have those types of friends out there. So, don't be afraid to offer something early on in the thank you page to entice hot buyers.

It flows like this - people will come to your landing page. They will give you their name and email address, and you will give them a gift for giving you their details. On the thank you page, you can either thank them and invite them to have a look through your website, to go to your Instagram, to go to your Facebook group if you have one, or your Facebook page. You can also test the waters and see whether they are actually going to be people who buy from you and offer them a low-end product—usually around $7 to $47 mark. Something that is sequential to the free thing you've just offered them. So, you might have offered them a PDF, and you'll offer them a video training on the thank you page for $47. This way, you can see who is red hot and who is actually ready to jump into bed with you.

Not all people will purchase from you straight away on that thank you page. That is more than alright because sometimes, some people need a few more coffee dates before they'll jump into bed with you. Online automated "coffee dates" are done through a simple nurture email sequence.

In the email sequence, it's really important you don't just jump straight into your offer, for two reasons. One is that a lot people will blacklist you as spam if you sell straight off the bat to them, and then your mail server will actually stop sending emails for you. This is really dangerous and I've had this happen to a client where she wanted to sell in her first three emails despite my warnings. Mailchimp shut her account down completely within a few days because too many people had said it was spam.

Put this in a face to face context. Say you're in line at Starbucks and the person in front of you was buying a latte and so were you. You notice that they're overweight. You rock up to them in the line and say "Hey, I notice that you're really fat. Do you want to buy my diet pills?"

Not cool! You would never, ever do that in real life—if you do, please put the book down, I'm not for you. But I'm assuming you're a person that likes to connect with other humans and are decent. If so, you'd probably have a chat with them and say, "Hey, getting a latte, too," and the person would say, "Yeah, I am, but I really don't want to have cream on the top because I'm trying to lose some weight. I'm doing really well. I've already lost 10kgs." Then you'd say, "Oh, wow, that's amazing! How have you done it?" They'd say, "Oh, mainly just through restricting calories" That's when you could pipe up and say, "Oh, wow! Cool! Well I've lost blah-blah weight and I think that it's fantastic. I use these pills, have you heard of them?" And that's how you can start to introduce your product. Much nicer way of talking about your offer without being pushy or offensive!

This is what I want you to think about when you write your email sequence. Too many people think that a long email sequence is just boring and that people won't read them and will hit delete. This may be true for some, but what I do know is the little bits that they do read of your email sequence will warm them up and let them know that you have been there before, you're the professional, and then have a special offer exclusively for them once they've used all of your free value and really got to know you.

This series of emails delivered one per day over the first week is what we call a nurture sequence. You want to nurture new people in to your community so they understand, trust, like, love, and just plain adore you. You can give away as much free stuff as you like within this free email sequence.

Once they adore you and binge watch everything you've ever made, you can send some sales emails in the sequence. You can offer them whatever it is you want to offer them because that is how you will be in service to them to go further in their journey. This is a very high-level, broad way of discussing this and if you want to get more granular and in-depth then please jump on over to the *Get Momentum Mastermind* where we actually spend a good few weeks going right through setting up your landing page, your thank you page, your value ladder, and also the five figure funnel that goes on the backend to ensure that you have the right way of converting these leads from cold into nice, warm, toasty buyers.

You may also wonder how you're going to drive traffic to your freebie—to extend your network beyond people you know. The fastest way to do this is through paid advertising. Now, you can and should always be doing organic outreach which is reaching out to friends and friends of friends. This is free but time inducive. If you want to hit your BIG dream goal and light a fire under your business then paid advertising is the fastest way of growing your business. But you must understand the numbers that are required.

A quick guide on what numbers to track can be found in the free bonus workbook with this book at www.pennyelliott.com/book

Advertising on the big behemoth, Facebook is easy and fast. You can have an add created and being sent out to 1,000's of people in less than an hour. The ease of use and immense targeting options have made Facebook ads popular with all. But don't discount Google Ads as they are coming down in price because of the competition in Facebook. Also YouTube ads are very exciting and new as well and one to master.

Just like any use of your money, paid advertising needs to be watched like a hawk. I do think that Facebook ads, I often say, are much like children. You need to watch them 24/7. Envision this-you sit your child down and they're happily playing away colouring. You step out of the room and empty the dishwasher. You come back and the children are drawing all over the walls and you think "what the fuck just happened?" This is exactly the same as Facebook ads, one minute the conversion cost is low and the next it sky rockets. Therefore it's very important that you understand how paid advertising works and what the structure is to optimise them.

During the $100K in 100 days challenge I spent NZ$14,000 on Facebook ads, which seems a lot. Yet I ended up making over US$100,000 dollars!

Sales = $100,000+

This is an investment I would do all day, every day. It's like going to the casino and putting a dollar in and getting a hundred dollars out every time you put it in. That to me is very exciting and a system to keep re-investing in. Bear in mind you don't have to spend $14,000 up front, this is something that's scalable and grows with your business. You can start an ad as low as $2 a day and scale from there. Having ads running 24/7 keeps filling up the sales pipeline, without you having to drive to any events at all!

If you're interested in knowing more about Facebook ads I haven't put the latest in the book; because as soon as this would have gone to print, it will be out of date. So, if you're interested, we have the up-to-date video training in the *Get Momentum Mastermind*.

Once you have an automated system in place to attract the leads and then an automated email sequence to show them love, value and eventually an offer you're set! You're ready to make $100k in 100 days. How exciting is that? Awesome!

GET MOMENTUM KEY POINTS

1. When you run out of bandwidth to grow your business from your network, it's time to take it online. An online presence increases your reach to a global audience.

2. Automation is key to helping your business grow while you're sleeping or spending time with your family.

3. Engage your audience slowly. Warm them up by providing value. That's how you build a loyal following that buys.

SECTION 3:

The Plan—
Matching the Woo with the Doo

Now that you know how to get your mindset into the right place—and you have all the leveraging techniques to get the Universe on board and manifest your dreams and desires within your business to crack that $100k in 100 days—you have the Woo. And you have the Doo-a tangible tool to create that wealth within the 100 days that you desire. Forevermore, you now have the sales skills to be able to sell in your business; because remember, if you don't have sales coming into your business, you just have a pretty Instagram account.

In this section, we're going to talk in granular detail about how to match that Woo with the Doo, because 80% of your business is mindset, and 20% is strategy. We're going to dive right in and find out exactly how you can bring about the right balance within your business. You're no longer going to work a crazy number of hours, and drive yourself into a hole of overwhelm. Those days of never actually seeing your family, or getting to that mid-day yoga are over. After all, that's precisely why you left your corporate job and decided to start your own business: to have freedom.

So, stayed tuned. In this section we talk about how to match the Woo with the Doo so that you can create your own freedom.

CHAPTER 16:

Focus and the Daily Ritual. The Woo Doo

It's well known that the area of your life where you focus your attention grows. For example, if you have a baby, or a kitten, or a cat, a puppy, or any sort of small dependable animal or child, you will know that the more you focus on them, and the more attention that you give them, they will grow. Not only physically in size, but mentally as well.

When you have a pet or a child, you cannot not put attention into them. Does that make sense? They are completely 100% dependable on you. You absolutely have to feed them, bathe them, clothe them, make sure they get sleep, give them a warm house and the stimulation to be able to grow from a baby to a toddler and into a young adult. You absolutely have to provide this focused energy; there's no choice around whether you show up as a parent or not. You can't just take the day off and hope they can fend for themselves. Every morning, they wake up and they need you, your attention, they need to be fed, and they need to be loved.

So, when it comes to your business, it always surprises me that people lose focus halfway. I see it regularly. Some days, clients are all in and do amazing amounts of work; the next day, they're haphazard. They'd say, "Oh, well, I'm a bit tired" or, "I did so much yesterday, I need to take a break today."

Often that break turns into a whole week. Now, we definitely want to be able to keep some balance in there so that you do take breaks, and we've talked in a previous chapter about keeping your wellbeing a priority. But focus in your business should be exactly like bringing up a child or your pet. You don't have a day off; you cannot lose focus. You must always be feeding your business with new leads and sales, you must be stimulating it with new opportunities and you need to have faith in yourself, every single day. You need focus on *both* the Woo and the Doo.

So many of my clients come to me and all they really want is the winning strategy. They want to know how to create a funnel, a sales page, and Facebook ads. Which is totally cool, I can do those things with my eyes closed. By the end of the coaching the one thing that changed the most in their business, or made the biggest shift in their business, is the Woo. The process of actually getting granular with their goals. It's getting into the journaling. It's getting into really letting their creative spirit come out and being able to take inspired action from that.

So, you need to be able to focus on both aspects—the Woo and the Doo—to be able to grow your business. You can't just journal once a week or meditate once every five days or go for a walk outside and really think about what you want to achieve in your business only when it's not raining. Alex Charfen famously calls them the primal walks, where you go out and you get really gritty with yourself, including in the rain!

You need to be doing these things daily to see lasting change.

So how to do balance the Woo with the Doo? My advice to all my clients and to you—as a valued part of my community and reader—is to focus on the money-making things in the morning. Okay? So, you can get up whatever time you like. You don't have to get up at the crack of dawn if you're not a morning person. That will only cause resentment for your business. If you love getting up at 5 AM, then go for it. If you don't and you'd rather sleep in, then go for it. That's why you've designed your business for freedom.

But what I do advise to all my clients and you is to start with the money-making activities in the morning. Now, I say this because as I said at the beginning of this section, if you don't have sales coming into your business, you just have a fancy Instagram account. You need to be making money to keep the wheels of your business turning. You need to be making money to keep your dreams alive. You need to be making money to keep the freedom in your life. While your energy is at its highest (in the morning), you need to focus on creating opportunities for the money to flow in.

If you have enough money to be able to pay for a cleaner, that gives you two hours a week back. If you have enough money in your life to be able to pay for really wonderful childcare, that takes the stress off your mind that your children are being looked after to the best standard, and you can actually crack on with more work or something that you want to do. If you're making great money in your business, you don't need to work fifteen hours a day; you just need to put in two effective hours every morning and spend the rest of the day on glide time. Yeah baby!

Then, I'd like you to spend the afternoon creating. Now, for some people, that might mean it's after the kids get back from school, they've done their homework, you've fed and bathed them, and then you do creation at night. It might be that you get up at 5:00, you've done your sales hours, and you start creating at 10 or 11 o' clock in the morning. All I'm saying is, do the creation *after* the sales.

Now, I would like to say—and some of my clients will be reading this, and they're probably saying, "No, that's not me." —99% of my clients start with the creation first. And it's natural. You're an entrepreneur, you have creative ideas, and that's why you've stepped out of your previous life and into this entrepreneurial world to be creative. What makes a great entrepreneur is having lots and lots of ideas and being able to bring them to fruition.

What also is a downer on having all this creation, is that we like to hide in creation mode. We love to create, create, create, create, create. Yet we don't love to sell, sell, sell do we? So many people—so many of my clients, too—have enough content to be able to give something away for free every single day of the whole year—without a shadow of a doubt. Yet, they need the sales to come into their business every single day of the year. As women, we shy away from money, we shy away from talking about sales, and we bring out that little girl voice. You now know how to get rid of those money blocks, and you now also have the Container Sale system, so you don't have to shy away from spending time making sales.

If you spend too much time in the creation zone you'll run out of time to do the sales, you're not putting any time into your money-making zone. This will then cause a roller coaster of money or clients coming into your business. You'll have a great time where you've put some focus onto sales, and then it'll drop straight off as soon as you've gone back into creation mode.

So, to stop you getting into creation mode, which can easily consume all of your time, you may be smiling to yourself if you think about how often you've looked at Facebook or Instagram today alone. (Shame on you – you're meant to be reading this book with full concentration!) Or you might have been creating a blog or an Instagram post, and all of a sudden, easily an hour has slipped by as you've really got in to it, "Ah, I need to tweak this and tweak that and make this colour look great, and that colour look great. Oops, that frame is too big. Mmm… what about this font?" You can easily lose a lot of time in creation. Which is a lovely, lovely place of flow to be in...once you've made your sales for the day!

Remember if you don't have money coming into your bank account, that creative flow feeling is not going to be any good to you when you wake up at 3:00 AM in the morning with the sweats thinking, "Shit. How am I going to pay for the bills?" or, "Oh my gosh, my poor husband has to go to work and do such long hours to support our family because I haven't sold anything." Or my particular favourite "Dam it, I need to sell somethings as my Credit Card is due this week….argggh" and then you can't sleep beating yourself up for not focusing on sales first.

By focusing on money first, it's just like my mother said. Well, actually, I'll tell you a story about it. I utterly hate peas. I absolutely **hate peas**. They are disgusting. I'm sorry to any pea lovers out there, but I think they're the spawn of the devil. They are horrible.

As a little four-year-old child, you can envision it now - long blonde hair right down to my butt, totally sassy attitude, only child - I was sitting at the dinner table, Mum said, "You need to eat your peas. Come on, eat your peas." I said, "I do not like peas." She replied, "You will eat your peas." I firmly said, "I will not eat my peas. I don't like peas."

Obviously I found my independence! Mum said, "You will eat your dam peas or you can't get down from the table." As the story is told to me I sat at the dinner table for nearly an hour. She even reheated the peas for me three times, trying to encourage me to eat them, but I would NOT eat them. Even my father came down from his home office and said, "Eat your peas, or there'll be discipline." I plainly said, "We'll let there be discipline, but I am not eating peas ever!"

The saga continued, mum even pulled the trick of "think about the poor children in less fortunate countries than you that don't have anything to eat." All I said was, "Well bring me an envelope, and I'll put the peas in, and we can post it to them, because I am not eating peas." You can imagine a little four-year-old skills throwing a solution-driven tantrum about not eating peas for an hour. I was finally let down from the table and I've never eaten a pea since. I have never been forced to eat peas again—it's quite a joke in our family. For year after mum used to always say to me is, "Eat your peas first." as an in-joke to eat the thing I hated the most first. Her reasoning was then you are left with all the other nice things on the plate leaving a yummy taste in your mouth last.

It is exactly the same with sales. Eat your sales peas first! Leave the yummy creation last. Sales activities can look like - outreach, sales calls, or it might be creating a sales funnel.

That then leaves you the whole afternoon and the rest of the evening—knowing that you have made money in the morning, or you've got money in the pipeline—leaving you all afternoon to be free, wild, and creative. Brilliant.

GET MOMENTUM KEY POINTS

1. Whatever you focus on, grows. Treat your business like a living, breathing creature that needs nurturing and total focus every day to grow and flourish.
2. Put in two effective hours first thing on sales activities. You need to be making money to keep the wheels of your business turning. You need to be making money to keep your dreams alive. You need to be making money to keep the freedom in your life.
3. Once you have made the money, you can do what you wish the rest of your day, including creating new and exciting things in your business.

CHAPTER 17:

Balance is Not 50/50

Most people think that strategy is all you need in business. You need to have a great marketing strategy, a great sales strategy, and obviously a fantastic product. This is true. However, when it comes to looking at your whole day, 80% of your business is your mindset and 20% is your strategy. Are you spending your day in this split? Probably not. Momentum starts with a solid mindset and then executing a solid strategy.

Many people have seen the controversial Fyre documentary on Netflix, where the main guy, Billy McFarland, used influencers to sell out an event that hadn't even been planned. One of the key factors that I took from many of the lessons in this documentary was that his mindset was solid.

All his staff said he was completely believable and honest. Interestingly he never took on a problem. He said to all of his staff, "We are not a problem business. We are a solution driven business." No matter what the issue that came up, and there were some pretty huge ones, his mind was rock solid on this amazing vision that he had to have this ginormous beautiful music festival. Because he held this vivid image and his mind was so set on it, an immense driving force was behind the festival going ahead. However in this case he didn't' have the Woo Doo balance; his strong mindset was actually undermining him. He had zero strategy. He just had the vision and the mindset to keep driving forward and bringing his people with him. The rest of the story you know, the festival was a failure and McFarland is now in prison.

Now, while I'm not saying you need to go about this Woo Doo balance exactly to this level, it is a very poignant documentary to understand that mindset will get you far greater in your business than hours spent on actual strategy.

I want to tell you a personal story about this. When I was in the pledge for $100k to 100 Days, I told my husband what I was going to do. He snorted and said, "Well I'm never going to see you am I?" I'd also entered the Ironman Taupo 70.3; a 1900-meter swim (1.2-mile), and then a 90km bike (56 miles), and then a half marathon at the finish. I wanted to train as hard as I possibly could for that all while being focused on my business goals. So, that meant I had to go cycling, and swimming, and running and do lots of training as well as chasing down this $100k goal.

At first, it felt really naughty when I went cycling in the middle of the day—you know, surely, I should be doing some more work? More sales – don't I teach that?! I should be working, working, working! Doing another sales activity, tweaking my sales pages, putting out another post.

The guilt arose from my corporate condition - my sales and marketing director role, my national sales manager role, my national sales account managers roles —all of these required me to be in the office, all of the day. So, to put all my cycling kit on and go out during the middle of the day while running my own business felt super naughty.

But this is where I find my greatest level of creativity. I have my best ideas when I step away from my laptop and put on my sports gear and get outside and feel that fresh air rushing through my hair and my veins. This is where my best business ideas flow. It's not forced. I'm not sitting at my desk thinking, "Right, what am I going to do? How am I going to do this?" I'm actually out in nature. My mind becomes clear. The left-right motion of either cycling, swimming, or running is actually meditative, and slows the brain to allow ideas to flow in.

The fresh air that flows into me is cleansing all those dusty cobwebbed ideas out of me despite it being a traditional working hour. Then, when I come back inside, I have huge amounts of inspired action because I've got all the blood pumping through my veins, I've sweated, and I'm ready to go. I work way more effectively than had I stuck inside and tried to grind it out.

You see, cycling in the sun brings me joy. When you do things that bring you joy, you come into your workspace with a much brighter aspect, than the stressed-out doldrums of being glued to your desk because this is what you think you *should* do to make it an effective work day.

You'll also do things much quicker, because you've actually had time to think them through. So, you won't make those mistakes that you do on the way through when you're tired and rusty. You avoid thoughts like, "Oh, God, now I've got to go right back to the beginning and start again." Or, "Oh, I mucked that up, so I need to go back and fix it."

So, to really Get Momentum in your business you need to reflect the 80/20 balance in your day. That might mean four hours of working each day and the rest is all play —doing things that bring you joy and working on your mindset. Now, you might think, "This is crazy. I'm never going to get anything done. I don't get everything done that I need to right now in the forty-plus hours I work." But I can tell you that I averaged 41 hours a week during the $100k in 100 Days challenge. I had one week that I did a fifty-hour week because the following week I was going away to the Gold Coast for a holiday, and so I needed to get a few things done. I didn't work on the weekends either, and I managed to average twelve hours of training every single week , throughout that 100 days. This shows you can have the space in your day for the Woo and follow through with your Doo to hit your big goals.

I want you to look at your calendar. Colour in your favourite colour for your work hours—I like to use green as green means go! Then colour your joyous activities in blocks a different kind of a really lovely bright colour. This could be reading, running, writing or relaxing. Whatever Woo activity that brings you joy.

In this visual representation, you'll be able to see your time allocations. Ask yourself - Am I actually spending more time working and less time joyous? Or am I spending 80% on that mindset, on that freedom, on focusing on joy, on journaling, on meditation, on yoga, on activities outside, on reading books, listening to podcasts, putting myself in the right vibe? Then 20% on the strategy, on the actual work? Try and get that balance every single week when you're having your meeting with yourself.

GET MOMENTUM KEY POINTS

1. You achieve balance when you realise that 80% of your business is your mindset and 20% is your strategy and your time allocation reflects this.
2. Spending time on what makes you happy will actually make you more productive.
3. Remember WHY you chose to start your own business.

CHAPTER 18:

Keeping consistent and persistent.

Making a success of an online business is all about being top of mind. This means you need to be consistent and persistent in front of your audience.

Most people understand consistent, which is like appearing in someone's inbox each week, or doing a Live stream every day. But persistent is a word that many female entrepreneurs really don't enjoy using, hearing, or being. They think it's very sleazy, slimy, and quite pushy. Well, I'm here to reframe that thought for you. When most people hear persistent in a sales context they're actually thinking of being pushy. Here's the difference between persistence and pushy: pushy is jamming something down someone's throat that they don't want; persistent is being present in someone's life with great value and support. That person who needs your services, and you know that having your special sauce will actually change their life for the better. Being persistent for them is in service to their goals.

Persistence, if you want to look at it in another way, is as follows. Say you go to the doctor and they tell you to lose weight because you're at risk of diabetes. They are not going to just tell you once; they're going to be very persistent, and keep calling you back, and telling you to come in for your tests. They're going to follow-up; they're going to get blood tests done, and they're going to be very persistent in telling you to lose weight and giving you all the opportunities to lose the dangerous pounds. Why? Because they are aware that your life is at risk and it is their duty to take care of you.

When you're thinking about being persistent with people, think about how their life is going to change through your product or services. It is your duty to care for them.

Consistency is the other half of the equation. Most people will say, "Oh, my product didn't sell" or, "Oh, I tried to launch a program and it didn't sell, so I'll try something else." First thing I ask is, "How many times have you spoken to your tribe, or your community about this product or service?" And they say, "Oh, I sent out one email," or, "I did one Live on it."

That's not being consistent. That is just showing up, asking for a sale, and then leaving again.

I was in a high-level mastermind with a lady called Rachel McMichael. She's a fantastic Facebook Ad and Website Agency owner, she has crushed it in an MLM company with over 7,000 in her team and now has The Business with Impact Society filled with wonderful woman. I'll never forget what she said to me one day, "What you see now is a reflection of what you did 30, 60, or 90 days ago Penny." It really struck a chord with me, I thought, "Wow. So true." Thank you, Rachel, for the enlightenment.

I knew this from my sales and corporate life, but didn't really see it in my own business until I got married at the beginning of March 2017. If you have organised your own wedding, you'll know that it is quite a lot of organisation. Doing everything on my own, I spent a lot of time—which is a luxury of owning your own business— organising my wedding.

When the sales kept coming in in February, I thought, "This is great, I can do both, yay". New clients kept flowing in March as well, which was fantastic. Then came April, and the new clients started to dry up. May was a very sparse month to put it politely. Actually I'm going to be open and honest about it; sales really plummeted and I thought, "What the F is going on?"

I looked back, and my sales activity 30, 60, and 90 days ago—particularly 60 days ago—was really poor. I was completely immersed in flowers, cakes, dresses, international guests arriving, and all the other dramas that go with getting married. The lack in money coming in didn't show up in the month of my wedding but sure did the months preceding the big day. This lesson really showed to me that if you hit those roller coaster moments in your business, it's because you're not being consistent and persistent in the months prior.

People need to see your face consistently, even if they're not ready to purchase. I'll give you another example of this fact. We bought our dream home—a seven-figure home overlooking a nature reserve and the ocean last year. Moving in was exciting, yet we needed to make some repairs, like you always do when you move into any house. I needed to find a plumber. I asked around, "Who knows someone? Who's got a really trusted plumber?" Over the next week or so I had a few people who referred their plumbers to me. While I was waiting for replies I went straight to my inbox, and thought, "Now, someone had sent me something about plumbing a while ago."

I just searched 'plumber' in my inbox search bar. Sure enough up popped several emails from a plumber. Now, if this plumber hadn't been persistent and consistent, either within my inbox, or someone else's inbox, I would not have chosen them or been referred them. The plumber had kept sending me emails and even though I wasn't in the market for a plumber before, I was now. By them being persistent and consistent through sending out value-led emails, I could easily find them, had already seen their results and felt comfortable reaching out to them to take on our home project.

Hopefully you can see this as an example that by consistently speaking to your list and your community you are being top of mind for when they're ready to purchase. Even if you're not getting the engagement back that you want straight away, know that the lifecycle of someone purchasing from you could be a lot longer than you desire. So, someone might be on your list for a year before they're going to purchase from you, or it might only be three days. It depends on how much pain they're in and how strongly they desire to get out of it!

So, stick to a day and time per week, and just send our an email. Every single week. No matter what, you must do it. Even if you're in the hospital, that will probably be the only time that you wouldn't need to, and you can schedule them out so that they are done in advance – no excuses! I have a client who is going away on a three-week holiday, and her whole social media and email content is all scheduled out, ready to go before she is. So, there is no gap in consistency and persistency. Therefore, in 30, 60, and 90 days' time, she will still have clients calls being booked, because she hasn't had this big glut of no action while on holiday.

Remember – you're the expert and the leader, so be dependable. This is the key ingredient to building the like, love, and trust within your community. It's all about the connections that you are creating. You know, if you have a reliable friend or an unreliable friend, who are you going to ask for help with something really precious? The reliable friend. Be the reliable person.

GET MOMENTUM KEY POINTS

1. The best way to be top of your leads' minds, is to be consistent and persistent even when they're not ready to purchase.
2. Your effort (or lack thereof!) will yield results in 30, 60 or 90 days.
3. Automation allows you to schedule communications well in advance, so there's no slump in activity if you need time away from your business.

Chapter 19:

Authenticity versus People-Pleasing

Something dear to my heart is people who are authentic, and actually don't give a flying fuck what other people think. Now, there's a difference between being a right bi-itch all over the Internet and being a right hot mess where you display everything, compared to someone who actually has an opinion and is able to back it up with some structure.

There's nothing worse than when you go into a clothing store and you try on a pair of jeans—why are jeans always the hardest thing to buy and find to fit? —and you look at yourself in the mirror and think, "Oh, my God! These are disgusting. I've got a huge amount of muffin top hanging over the top. I can barely fit down in them, and they make my hips look like a whale, and it is gross." Just as you're about to have a complete meltdown in waltzes this shiny sales assistant, and she gushes, "Oh, my God, they look amazing. Those jeans look so gorgeous on you." And you think, "That is a load of B.S. There is no way these look gorgeous."

Girlfriend - you're not being attention-seeking by thinking this; you just know damn right that they are dreadful. You take them off, and you leave and you think, "This isn't even gonna work."

Compare that to the sales assistant who's bright and shiny, and comes in and goes, "Ooh, they look a bit snug. Would you like me to get you the next size up? While I'm at it, I have another pair that has deeper pockets, so they make everyone's butt look smaller," and, "Would you like to give them a go?"

Although this sales assistant hasn't stroked your ego and erred on the side of truthful, you're gonna think "authentic", too. She is there to help you find a pair of jeans that suits your body shape and looks fab. Once you try on the bigger size and the deeper pocket style you look ace, no more muffin top! You don't even worry about the price (or the bigger size!), because you know that they're helping you buy the right pair of jeans that you can confidently strut your stuff in. This is the difference between being a people-pleaser or truly authentic in your sales. Unfortunately, in the online world, there are so many people trying to be people-pleasers and not very much authenticity.

Think about the Fyre Festival and the documentary that revealed all. They were trying to create this festival and please people by having all different accommodation options that seemed completely amazing. Yet they were completely inauthentic about it because behind the scenes they just could not produce even 10% of what they were promising. So, when you are finding your voice online, make sure that you are being the person that you want to be known as forever. Be authentic, it might ruffle feathers of those who don't agree but it is better than trying to be friends with everyone and failing.

So, if you don't fly on a private jet, do not talk about flying on a private jet. If you don't drive a Bentley or even a BMW, do not have a photo standing in front of a Bentley, all dolled up, thinking this is the life that you're going to create for others. This kind of in-authenticity is very, very easy to research and find out if you're faking it. It only takes one troll and your business will all come crashing down, very, very quickly. As we saw in the Fyre Festival, it only takes one or two tweets to go viral for a whole, huge, million-dollar branding exercise to come crashing down and end up in jail.

So, make sure you're authentic.

Now, finding your authentic voice is, and can be a long journey. It also changes as you develop your ideas and your thoughts. That's more than OK.

I have a very close friend who wants to be on the spiritual side more, and she's growing into her spirituality as a coach. She's growing into her money mind set work as a coach. She has now grown into fully being a mindset and universally lead coach. Had you asked her eighteen months ago what she was going to do, she would have said business coaching, in fact Amazon coaching for Mums. You may have seen her—Noor

Hibbert; she now has a book out called *Just Fucking Do It* which is all about manifestation and nothing to do with products on Amazon. Finding your voice is evolving, and that is OK. Yet, being authentic through the process is key.

It's about being vulnerable about your hard times, and showing the lessons that come from that. Show why you're changing tack and evolving and bring your audience along with you. This is how people will connect with you deeply and eventually want to work with you. So, you don't have to be all rainbows and unicorns, bright, shiny, and fluffy for people to really enjoy and connect with you. It's actually the opposite. The more you show your authentic stuff, the more connection you are going to have with people.

GET MOMENTUM KEY POINTS

1. Authenticity is about having a voice and backing it up with structure.
2. Be the person who gently corrects someone else, rather than lying to them to please them.
3. You don't have to be a hot mess for people to be drawn to you. Just be authentic.

CHAPTER 20:

Tracking your Numbers and Mini-Celebration

It's so important to know where you've come from, to be able to know how far and how advanced you have become. It's too easy to be stuck in the now and comparing yourself to others further along. Yet you don't know what's behind their closed doors. So, it is a fake comparison and one that will eat you up and spit you out in a place that's negative.

A far better and more positive place is to see just how far you've come. Often, we focus on the next thing, the next thing, the next thing, and never take stock on just how far we've come. It's very important that you track your numbers so you can see them growing. Below is an example of how my numbers grew, to be completely transparent, throughout the $100k to 100 Days. People will often just focus on the end goal of $100k, and rarely think, "Wow, I'm 30% through, or I'm half way - yay," and be really pleased and show gratitude for where they've come from.

Most people will just wait for their big goal to be achieved and then have a glass of champagne or go out for dinner, instead of celebrating all the mini-wins along the way. I'll never forget, my first coach told me that a glass of bubbles didn't really cut it when she'd finally reached the goal. Instead, she decided to celebrate all the mini-wins on the way. This keeps you in a high vibe state and pressing forward for the big goal.

So, for example, if you're launching a new product, it's not just about when the product launches or when the product hits a $100k in sales. It's about all the little steps along the way.

For example, I celebrated the mini steps in creating *Get Momentum Mastermind*. Every masterclass that I created within the membership area—there's 15 of them, plus some bonuses-I celebrated. I'd do some fist pumps and say "Yes, that's another amazing masterclass that's going to transform someone's life and change the way that they see the world. It's going to help some lucky woman get momentum in the way that they do business and transform their bank accounts." I'd have a fancy cup of tea (I was pregnant so no bubbles for me) and have a mini lie down and read a book. For every masterclass that went in to that membership area, I'd have a mini-celebration. I didn't wait until I had finished the whole course, and then sit down and go, "Ah, wonderful," and have a glass of (non-alcoholic) wine. I celebrated along the way as well as at the end to keep me motivated and cherishing the mini milestones to achieving the great, big milestone.

Now, I remember being told, "Celebrate the mini-wins on the way" and I thought, "Gosh, there's so many mini-wins on the way, I'm going to turn into an alcoholic." So, celebrating doesn't always have to be a glass of bubbles—although that is good fun. It can be sitting back and reading a book for an hour, guilt-free, knowing that this is your treat for having completed one of your mini-goals. It might be that you go for a walk. It might be that you take the afternoon off. It might be that you sit in the bath and light a candle, even though you don't have a romantic setting or a fancy bathroom. You just light a candle and you think, "This is just for me." Or it might be that you sleep in a bit longer one morning, a special favourite of mine while pregnant! Anyone else find sleep so glorious?!

It can be an easy, cheap, free celebration. But celebrating all those mini-goals along the way is going to make it so much sweeter when you hit your goal, because one glass of bubbles doesn't cut it when hitting your big goal that you've worked months towards. Trust me. It'll seem so insignificant when you get there.

Celebrating only once isn't the right positive feedback loop, that you're looking for to get momentum either. You want to be able to celebrate as you go, so that you feel the joy of completing a task. This joy creates continued enthusiasm to keep going, which in turn gives you the motivation to tackle the next task. You then see the success of completing that task. Which gives you the confidence to keep going. Feeling confident that you're going on the right path brings joy in what you're doing every day and the flywheel of momentum keeps going. As this flywheel keeps spinning, this is how you get yourself to a high level of productivity, engagement, and eventually sales and money in your bank account.

If you only celebrate once every couple of months when you hit your dream goal, or even once a year when you look at your numbers for the tax man, then the motivation and excitement can get very low throughout the year, which means that you could actually become demotivated and miss your goal completely.

By tracking your numbers daily, weekly or monthly enables you to make the adjustments and alterations early on so that you can hit your big goal numbers. You can also see just how far you've come, because you might not hit your goal the first time around. But if you've tracked your numbers, you'll be able to see how close you're getting. You might even surprise yourself and be further ahead than you thought you were. By having the data you can do more of what is working well and cut out what isn't.

A great example is Denise Duffield-Thomas, the amazing woman behind Money Bootcamp. She sold three people into her first course, she just sold 360 into the same course this time round, five years later. Now, if she hadn't tracked her numbers, she wouldn't recognise this HUGE increase and success. If she hadn't celebrated those three people in the beginning, she probably wouldn't have had the momentum to keep going and hit 261 people this time round. Imagine all those women's lives that she is changing, helping them understand their money better, and being able to be at ease with money in their lives, all by celebrating her mini wins and then looking at her numbers, making changes and keeping on going. This is a perfect example of how knowing how far you've come will get you to where you want to go.

So, keep celebrating. Jump into the free workbook at www.pennyelliott.com/book for a list of ideas for mini-celebrations for you. Pick one, take a picture of you celebrating and make sure that you pop it up on Instagram @penny_elliott_ so I can see your win!

GET MOMENTUM KEY POINTS

1. Celebrate all the small wins along the way to your dream goal.
2. A celebration doesn't have to be big or expensive. It's about self-love and appreciation.
3. Track your progress by knowing your numbers in your business so you can be grateful for your growth and keep doing what is working.

SECTION 4:

Keeping Momentum

Often, you'll read a book like this with huge amounts of excitement and desire. If you're anything like me you've highlighted paragraphs, written in the margins and taken inspirational shots and put it to your Insta Stories (remember to tag me @_penny_elliott_ so I can share you too!)

Once you've finished you put the book down and you think, "This is great. I'm going to get this all in place." And then, give or take three or four days, and you go back to your own ways. Along comes the children, along comes your husband, along comes another great movie. Netflix releases a new documentary, or Marie Kondo does another series... Suits comes along... The cat needs to go to the vet, and all of a sudden, you've lost several months and not implemented anything.

You haven't reached $100k in 100 days, and you haven't gotten to where you wanted to go when we first started this book—where you started with the end in mind. You might be thinking, "Oh bollocks, I failed to do what Penny suggested!"

So, then you pick up another book, and you go down the path of trying that theory.

And, again, the cycle continues.

Without implementation your dream goal will not come to fruition. In this section, I want to talk about how you can take the action TODAY and keep momentum going so that you can reach your $100k in 100 days. It's up to you and I believe in you. You can do this, it's starts with you and now.

CHAPTER 21:

What Went Wrong and
How to Overcome It?

Where did it all go wrong? Now, I'm not going to say that everything in business is fancy lunches, glamorous photo shoots and fancy retreats. There are crap days, there are crap moments, and there are crap seasons. But it is up to you, your mindset, the woo, and the strategy you put in place, the doo, to keep yourself moving forward.

Keeping momentum is all about having the excitement to do the action and the excitement to get the results, which includes changing your mindset when things don't go as planned. You're in charge of moving around, and around, and around the Get Momentum Fly Wheel, no matter what setbacks you have. Even if you know the outcome wasn't unfair, wasn't your fault or you feel like the world is against you.

So, when you think about what went wrong in your business, most coaches will say, "Don't focus on the wrong. Focus on what went right." But, I wanna be realistic here.

Things go wrong.

And, it is up to you to identify where they went wrong, and then put into place the positive changes needed to make it go right next time. This is a positive outcome versus wallowing in self-pity or blaming everyone else.

Some of my clients have things that go wrong in their business while we're working together. That doesn't mean that I'm not a good coach, or that they're not a diligent client, and don't run a good business. It is just the nature of business. The path is not always a straight line up and up.

However the woman who wins in business know how to identify where parts went wrong, put a stake in the sand, and create the wrongness as a lesson to be learnt from. This is the key - there's actually nothing that is wrong. It's all just lessons that you need to learn, but if you don't identify them first, you'll never know and grow.

Is it that you lost your daily practice? So, let's go back to a daily practice and make it a priority right after you go for a wee in the morning. Start small—aim for a minute a day so it's achievable and you get back in to a routine.

What is it that you need to do every day to get your head clear and in the right space to create inspired action in your business? Is it that you need to do more meditation? Or maybe your meditating for 30 minutes and then have no time to journal out those amazing ideas. Do you need to lower your meditation down to allow for more journaling time?

Do you need to start acting like the woman that you want to be? If so, put on some lippy each day to bring your mood up. Perhaps you go and look at some dream homes on the weekend to raise your vibration. Or drag out the fancy jewellery that is reserved for special occasions and strut round the house in. Get your diamond freak on girl!

Has your exercise routine gone out the window and your energy levels slumped? Ask yourself – when was the last time you got outside and sweated? If the answer is any longer than the day before then you're well overdue for some outside connection to Mother Earth. Get your butt outside, no matter the work load.

Be honest…has your eating slipped back into fast foods and stuff on-the-go? Time to get focused again, pick foods that nourish your soul and your creativity? It's not about depriving yourself, it's about fuelling your best asset – yourself! You wouldn't accept a staff member coming to work for you hung over each day and having takeaways piling up on her desk would you? Food for thought there!

Have you stopped using your essential oils? How can you bring them back in to your routine, especially during your sales hours earlier in the day. Perhaps you get a diffuser and it goes on before you open your laptop with your favourite oil.

Have you let other people into your life that have penetrated that solid mindset that you had when you first started this book and did the homework? Have they started to eat away at you and cause doubt? If so, kick 'em to the curb. Not literally, but distance yourself as much as you can. Choose the option to silence them on your social apps so you're not tempted to check out what they're up to. They will never know either. Decline any social occasion with the dream goal vampires too and give yourself the space to get strong again on your dream goal.

If any of these things have happened, I'd like you to go back to the first section of this book, The Woo and read it again. Commit to your daily practice. Commit to your exercise. Commit to identifying your money blocks. These things are not a one and done exercise. They're a continuous effort as you move forward through the stages of your business and self-growth.

When I started doing Ironman training, I committed 100%. I hired myself a coach. I hired a nutritionist. I went to a sports psychologist. I surrounded myself with the right type of people. I was all in. That first Ironman went so smoothly; I was so pleased. I couldn't believe how awesome the experience was. I was hooked, and subsequently, I've entered seventeen more Ironman's and completed them all. But along the way, I did lose my determined focus. As a result some races went worse rather than better. I made a lot of mistakes. The night before Ironman UK I had a glass of wine, not sticking to my pre-race meal at all. I paid the price as I then had the shits the next day in the race—TMI probably, sorry.

Ironman Germany I didn't check my tires correctly one, and I ended up having several flat tires and running out of spares.

I had to ride the last 12km on the wheel rim which completely ruined my fancy carbon wheel set, an expensive mistake.

At Ironman Lanzarote, the hilliest race on the circuit, I didn't check my rear derailleur—a little mechanism on the back of the bike—when I screwed it back on after flying and I can tell you right now, if that doesn't work, your bike doesn't work. On one of the big climbs it started to come loose and cost me at least thirty minutes as it fell off and I had to wait for mechanical assistance. All because I was being complacent. I had lost my daily focus. I had lost my drive and attention to the small details.

I want you to be ok with the fact that sometimes things slip. You're human, so no beating yourself up. Instead use that energy to go back through this book and identify where you need keep being consistent. Keep noticing your conscious language to others and yourself, keep developing your confidence in saying your offer, and keep identifying money blocks as they come up.

Which leads me onto the next thing that commonly pops up and halts woman growing businesses: money blocks as you grow. You might have identified all your money blocks at your current situation. People often say your bank account is only a reflection of where you are right now. So, that is true, but most people only use this saying if they have nothing in their bank accounts or are in huge credit card debt.

So, say you've got zero in your bank account right now, then that's a reflection of where you are right now. But say you have $100,000 in your bank account; that's also a reflection of where you are right now, and sorry to say but new money blocks come up at this new level too.

As one of my coaches, Emily Williams famously said, "New levels, new devils." Once you have the $100k in your bank account you might get thoughts of worry about how you'll keep it there and not spend it. Or will this wealth and growth last? You then make a wrong turn and boom, it's all gone. This wasn't a wrong strategic business decision but more than likely a money block you have that needs to be healed so that you can sit comfortably with this new level of wealth in your bank account.

You need to continuously check on your money blocks to keep moving forward. Otherwise, you might reach a level where you feel comfortable, and you'll stay there. No matter how much you try to move forward, you'll self-sabotage to stay in your comfort zone.

Create a new set point within yourself. You need to decide, "Right, okay. Now, I'm the woman that makes $100,000 in 100 days. What are my new money blocks around this? Do people think that I'm going to be snooty? Do I have to now drive a certain car, have a certain house, have a certain handbag? What does that mean about me?"

What are these blocks within you? Is it that you now feel that you need to give back when really you don't have the time to give back yet? Keep exploring and releasing them through the journaling exercises or EFT daily.

Tapping needs to be done daily. Usually, people love it soo much to start with and dive in boots and all. They see instant results. High on the new results they then don't have time to do it daily, and I completely understand that. I often get so excited about the next great project, like this book, that I forget all the stepping stones that got me here. But it's important not to neglect your energy. Therefore to keep it daily you don't have to do the full seven-point tapping, you can actually use the side of your fingers for a quick tap out.

Interestingly this is where most people end up rubbing their hands or biting their fingernails when they're nervous; because this is where the meridian lines run as well. You can easily tap with your thumb on all four fingers. Just keep moving through them and saying your affirmations. You can easily do this while you're driving, sitting in traffic, waiting in line, or on the loo. There is always a place where you can do a quick EFT session and help move those money blocks.

If your Woo is rock solid then things might be going wrong as you don't have the Doo dialled in. Perhaps you don't have enough leads coming in. Reflect to yourself, what have you been doing to put yourself out there? Have you really been visible to your ideal client or have you been in creation mode and silent to the outside world? Have you really been connecting with people or just focusing on patting your cat each day? Be honest with yourself and then make a plan to pick up the connect again. it's very easy to say, "Oh, I've done it all. I've done it all" … But when it comes down to it, if you don't have leads coming in, then you don't have the right strategy in place. Commit to being seen online every day for the next month.

You need to be honest with yourself and think about what you did 30 days ago. What did I do 60 days ago? What did I do 90 days ago? Now look to see if there was a gap. Did you stay persistent and consistent in your communities mind?

If there is a gap, don't beat yourself up, simply ask "How is that reflecting now in the fact that I don't have any leads? What can I do to perk that up quickly?"

If you're a bit stuck, don't' worry you're not the only one. I used to coach athletes who were time-restricted. These people worked in high-profile jobs, but really wanted to be able to do a half-marathon or a marathon. So, their training schedule would be different to someone who could just get something out of a book. They had extremely limited time, and so needed their training to be able to work efficiently and effectively. It also needed to be pencilled in with their P.A., so that they would have the time and space to complete the workout.

With all this specification set for them each week, they'd often tell me, "Oh, I didn't do this run, and I didn't do that run, oh and I didn't quite get to do this one either."

And I would say to them, "Look…"

They'd quickly interrupt me; "I'm sorry! I still really want to do a two-hour half-marathon."

I would say to them, "I'm sorry, but the race organisers are not bringing the finish line any closer to you. How do you expect to get round the 21kms if you don't train?"

Harsh I know. But if they haven't actually done the work, then when it comes to the race day, they're gonna be exposed. The race finish line isn't going to be brought closer to them just because they didn't get to do their long runs, right?

It's the same in business. You'll be completely exposed if you have no clients, or your product launch isn't how you hoped to be. It will be no-one else's fault. It won't be because Facebook declined your ads or Active Campaign sent all your emails out at once. Because all these things can be worked around. As I told my athletes "If you really want to get to the finish line, then you'll put in the training, even if it means getting up at 4am." Or in the case of business – creating a new ad account and loading up new ads, sending out an apology email and continuing on.

What can you do more to support your launch, design a new product, give the service that is needed to get out there? What is it that you need to do to feel physically alive and really smash out some inspired action? How can you step out of that comfort zone and create and cultivate the confidence that you need to have to do the work to hit your goal dream?

Answers to all these questions will then lead you to inspired action. Just as you need daily Woo, you need to take daily inspired action—which is the Doo. Find out what your ideal client wants right now. This might have changed since you first asked them and that's why your product is falling on deaf ears. Really find out what their pains are and help them see that you can solve their pain and take them to the pleasure state they so desperately want.

If it's going wrong check in with your vibe and tone. Are you feeling a bit low? Then it's time to bring that vibe right up again! Always come prepared and high vibe. Whatever shit is going on in your life is left at your office door as you make yourself ready and available for your tribe.

Are you trying to be like someone else? Be your authentic self. Make sure you get yourself out there in an authentic way, and then it won't be difficult or false-which people can sense a mile off. This might be putting them off you and a reason why no-one is working with you. Check in on yourself.

Is it that you don't know where to find your clients? Now, I get this a lot with a lot of clients. They say, "Oh, I don't know where they hang out." There's a real fear around actually getting gritty with your ideal client and snooping on their online activities. You need to take the guesswork out of knowing your clients right at the beginning, because getting gritty with them is going to make it so much easier for your sales in the long run. Yet, a lot of woman shy away from this key activity.

I know when I first had to do market research, I thought it was so boring, hearing the same thing over and over from different women. When I saw the resistance in other women, I thought it was for the same reason. But I found out the reason why a lot of women shy away from getting gritty with their ideal clients is because they actually had to get on the phone and ask questions of other people. The mere thought was terrifying for them. But you must put on your inspector hat and really get gritty and understand this other person you're trying to sell to or else all your hard work of creating the offer and marketing it will fall on ears that don't want it. Now, that would be a shame and a big place to go wrong.

If calling people to ask questions makes you sweat, then I want you to take a moment and spend some time journaling around this feeling. Then dig into finding that confidence within yourself to be able to ask these questions and see it as being in service to the millions of people ahead of you. Find out what they like and what they don't like, what they read and watch and who else they hang out with. Because once you know where your clients are, it's gonna be a whole lot easier to tap into them, and you won't be swimming in a ginormous sea. You'll actually be in your little pond with all your hungry fish.

Is it that you're not converting on your sales pages or on calls? Now, this is a huge problem that I see with a lot of people online having. They are too quick to slap up a sales page, and they don't put any time or effort into it.

Russell Brunson is a fantastic mentor in all sales page education. He spends hours and hours—sometimes days— working out just the title, the hook, catch, and phrase. He then moves on to the rest of the sales page and goes in to huge amounts of depth of what the buyer will get. Even though he is a huge icon and people already know and trust him he goes to this effort to explain every little bit.

All the way through your sales pages you want what I call nodding dogs. You know those little dogs that are in the back of the car that nod up and down as you drive—like yes, yes, yes? You do this by being warm and inviting all the while really digging into the pains of your ideal customers. They must feel as though you're speaking directly to them, even if you're only selling a $5 product. You absolutely have to talk about their pain and pleasure points, and you have to know what their buttons are. That way, you can coax them to push your button to make their purchase.

If you want your sales pages to shine, you can't slap them up once and think you're done. You have to continuously tweak and improve your sales pages as more and more traffic sees it. The more data you have the more you can fine tune the page to increase your sales.

If your Call to Action (CTA) is to have sales calls and you're getting calls booked but it's going wrong on the call, then I can now strongly recommend that you go back to the Container Sales chapter and reread that. Practice, practice, practice, practice. Practice makes perfect.

Remember when you were first learning to drive? I know I found it difficult. I learned in a manual car, and you had to put the clutch in and change gears, look in the rear-view mirrors, keep looking forward, hold the wheel straight; let the clutch out, and put the accelerator down, and hope like hell it didn't bunny hop and stall where you'd have to start all over again. It was very stressful.

I kept thinking how on Earth am I going to do this? How will I actually move the car forward smoothly and change gears? And I remember always getting through all the gear changes and into the top gear and thinking, "Oh, my gosh! I just hope I can drive the whole way to where I'm going in this gear, because then I'm not going to have to change gears again."

I was petrified of changing gears. But with a huge amount of practise and by about professional lesson number five or six, I had the hang of changing gears. The stress was much lower and I didn't need to panic about getting to my destination in top gear only. Now, I can drive without even thinking about my feet moving or what gear I need to be in. It just naturally happens. This is what I want you to get to your sales calls.

You need to be able to know your Container Sales inside out, so that it feels natural. It must feel like it's an everyday conversation, and the only way that you're going to get this, is through practice. Practice, practice, practice!

Now, you don't want to be practicing with live leads—people who actually need your support. You want to be practicing with people that can give you feedback. So, make sure you jump into the Get Momentum Entrepreneurs Facebook group, and write a post asking for somebody who can be a role-play buddy with you. That way, you both can have a turn at being the sales person and then give each other feedback. There will be others within the group that are looking for this as well so don't be shy!

The other place I see sales calls going wrong, is when clients don't have a lot of sales calls booked into their diary each week. When they are on a precious call there is a lot of pressure to convert every single one of them to make bank for the month. Now, I'd love to say that a 100% conversion rate is possible, and it is. However, there will always be someone who doesn't want to buy from you, despite how much you nurture them. Also, if you're getting a 100% conversion rate, your prices are probably too low for what you're product or service.

You definitely will have some people say no to you, and you know what? A no just means not right now. It doesn't mean no forever. So, you need to firstly, be okay with that. Secondly, realize that if you have five calls in your diary for the week, it will not necessarily equate to five instant sales. Release the pressure on yourself to make this happen. Once you've done that, it will be a whole lot easier and you'll project a much more confident nature. Not one of desperation.

Another thing to consider is not to bring your money desires to the call. Don't get in the mind trap of thinking, "Well, if I sign this gal up, I'll spend the money on my FB ads, my mortgage, and my car repayment." This kind of pressure means that you're not going to be in service with people on the call. You're actually going to be just pushing for the sale no matter what. You lose your authenticity to serve, and that will turn a whole lot of people off. When you're just thinking about what you're going do with that money, that means that you are not listening to the other person. You're not trying to think of the best solution for their needs; you're just trying to get the sale to fulfil your needs. Take a good look at yourself and think about what's happening before and on the calls.

To help evaluate yourself I recommend that you record your sales calls and listen back to them afterwards. Don't only listen to the words you use, but the tone and pitch too. Try to detect if there's any desperation in your voice whatsoever. Are you really listening?

Another place where I see woman going wrong on sales calls is when they're giving away too much. People are actually thinking, "Wow, this is amazing. I've got all the help, and encouragement or coaching I need now. I don't actually need to buy the product. I'm all sorted!"

Stick to the Container Sales method, and you will be in service to the person in taking them to the next level, which is either making a decision to be yes or no with you. You will be in service to them on the call without giving away everything. You'll have lovely clients and a lovely bank balance.

And remember, when things go wrong in your business, it is just a lesson to learn from and then get back in to momentum.

I hope you really enjoyed this book, *Get Momentum*. I'd really love to hear how your journey is going, and the amazing sales that you've hit. Tell me how you've created momentum in your business and how you're creating $100k in 100 days.

Please pop on over to the Facebook group *'Get Momentum Entrepreneurs'* where you can share your message or pop it in an Instagram Story and tag me @penny_elliott_

Thank you very much for taking time to read this book, and I wish you all the best in the Woo and the Doo in your journey to $100k in 100 Days.

**If you need some more support and help in your business, then the *Get Momentum Mastermind* is the melting pot for you. Pop on over to www.pennyelliottgroup.com/GMM and jump on a call with us. We'd love to give you a free strategy session to help iron out the bits you're not so sure on and if you're the right fit, invite you in to the mastermind. Talk soon lovely xxx

Your New Manifesto

I live my life by Getting Momentum! I build my business with passion and creativity AND I take time out for ME. I play, I have fun and I LIVE! I create impact in the world by serving others, and I am an influencer among my family, friends, and community. I don't complain about what I can't change. Instead, I take action and make things happen!

I look after my body and mind so I can serve more people on a higher level.

I don't hustle and grind; I create targeted sales action to create WORLD impact!

I invest in myself and my business to grow my reach. My sales-savvy ways create a flow of money that frees me to relax and enjoy life. I Get and Keep Momentum!

Acknowledgements

I've always wanted to write a book, haven't we all? But the fire didn't burn bright enough until someone said to me 'how come you haven't got a book with all your years' experience in media, is it because you're not good enough?'. Being asked if I'm not good enough is like a red rag to a bull to me. The fire was lit and it has burned for a year now to get this out to your hands, because I am good enough!

Many people have helped keep the fire alive when I was occupied trying to navigate the first year of motherhood, keep the house running and my business alive. To them I am forever grateful.

I would never have been able to write on this topic and my journey without the help, coaching, guidance and love of Christina Jandali. Easily one of the most loving and talented woman on the planet-god did good in creating this one. I would never have embarked on the coaching journey without the consistent and persistent marketing of Emily and James Williams and joining their coaching program-I Heart My Life.

I have surrounded myself with like-minded people throughout the journey – Lise Cartwright, Rachel McMichael, Noor Hibbert, Becs Button, Anna Powers, Kim Heintz, the

Mastermind Babes; Louise Blakely, Larissa Macleman and Sarah Quinney. Jennifer Mayes – nothing technical would happen without you! Chris Benetti, Kim Barrett and Deb Malone for the sweetest funnels and ads to make sure the sales happened!

I wrote and recorded much of this book while taking my wee bubba Joshua on walks, anything to make them sleep right? When I was at wits end on how to do the next stage of babism the Yogi Bears were always there to help. I couldn't have done it without you Jess, Missy, Rebecca, Laura, Greer, Lene and Pip.

To all my athletic coaches and team mates – you showed me what tough was. How to be gritty and just get it done. The Ironman journey shaped my life and you were all a huge part of that journey. The book isn't long enough to name you all, that might need to be a whole new book...but Sarah, Nicole, Mia, Andrea, Kerry, Liz, Eleanor, Christina, Renatta, Graeme, Paddy, Nick, Dave, Vince and all the Fulon-Tri crew and Marina, Fiona, Michelle, James, Tommy and the Hit it or Quit it squad – you're forever in my heart and head when I want to quit. Which was lots getting this to print!

Lastly my wee family. I am an only child, of an only child, and I now have only one child. We keep it tight! Mum and Sam you've always supported my crazy adventures never really knowing what I was up to. I'm sorry I'm not a farmer like you both, but I think I've taken on your kick arse sales and business skills that you taught me by leading by example every single day and put them to good use. You'll always be my best example of doing what you love and making good coin, every single day.

I know once Scott, my husband, sees this printed in his hand he'll be proud and realise I wasn't just saying I was going to do it, but actually doing it! See, I wasn't watching Netflix in the middle of the day!

Joshua – you were with me the whole way writing this, mainly asleep. Unbeknown to you, you are my driving force for empowering mum's a-like to have the confidence to get momentum in their lives and business so they can be with their little ones more. Love you more everyday monkey.

Finally – to my amazing grandparents. Grammy and Poppy you were my rocks and none of the opportunities I have had in life would have been as colourful without you. Keep watching over me.

About Penny Elliott

Penny lives and breathes sales; from selling grapes on the side of the road in her family business at age 7 right though to leading teams of 45 sales reps throughout the UK, culminating in over $15 million dollars' worth of sales in her twenty years in the corporate world. Now running her multiple 6-figure business for the past four years, she cuts through the shiny objects to show her clients how to attract leads, build relationships, create buyers, profit, and growth in her clients' businesses.

Keeping a balance is key to Penny and her clients; she lives and breathes this, having completed 18 Ironmans, including the World Champs and over forty marathons. She loves to write and has been published in over thirty publications all while being a wife, crazy Bengal cat lady, and mum.

Penny is on a mission to help you *Get Momentum—the Woo with the Doo*: The perfect mix of mindset and strategy to have fast success in your business so you can finally live your best life.

Made in the USA
Middletown, DE
10 January 2020